GOD'S REVOLUTION AND MAN'S RESPONSIBILITY

GOD'S
REVOLUTION
AND MAN'S
RESPONSIBILITY

harvey cox

THE JUDSON PRESS, VALLEY FORGE

107834

BR
123
.C72

CONTENTS

Preface 7

God's Revolutionary World 13

Sin: Man's Betrayal of His Manhood 37

The Gospel: God's Word for His World 51

Sacrament: Suffering with God in His World 77

Ministry: Working with God in His World 101

PREFACE

Most of this book grew out of the lectures I delivered at the annual Baptist Student Conference at Green Lake in August, 1963. I mention this somewhat prosaic temporal fact in the unlikely event that some future historian of ideas might wonder how the thoughts expressed here could grow out of my book *The Secular City* (New York: Macmillan, 1965). The answer is, of course, that they did not. They preceded them. I gave these lectures just after I had returned from a year in Berlin, Germany, serving as a fraternal worker with the Gossner Mission. Just a few days before I gave the lectures I had participated in the historic March on Washington for Jobs and Freedom on August 28, 1963. Many of the students had also been there and the conference was fairly jumping with the spirit of the freedom movement and crackling with

7

keen controversy. The lectures rightly reflect the buoyancy and hopefulness of that wonderful summer in American history.

This is not to say that I would change anything now in the more serious and deliberate mood of 1965. I would not. I still feel that the biblical God calls man through events of social change, and that the church becomes the church by participating in the revolutionary work of God.

However, if I were writing these lectures over today, I might feel it necessary to clarify some of the fairly bald and assertive prose, or at least to relate it to some of the more current theological debates. I would want to explain why, for example, I still blithely use the term "God" in an age when some theologians are insisting that he is dead. I use the old appellation, *i.e.*, "God," not because I think it is totally unambiguous but because I think it can be saved from its current ambiguousness and emptiness only if it is employed in markedly altered contexts and in radically new ways. This is the way the meaning of words is changed and renewed.

I think those who feel that "God" is dead have already gone over to the side of traditional theism or classical metaphysics and then merely stood the whole business on its head. They accept an antiquated orthodox definition of who God is, and then merely disagree on the question of whether he is still alive. I would prefer to differ with the orthodox at a more basic level of the argument and insist that the God they say is alive and the others say is dead is just not God. In the epochal words of Kierkegaard, "Hear ye, hear ye, the God of the philosophers is not the God and father of our Lord Jesus Christ." The term "God" will regain currency in modern speech only if we use it in such new and jarring ways that its old meanings are cracked and discarded. Hence, "God's Revolution."

Readers of my book entitled *The Secular City* will also note an element of brashness and arbitrariness in *God's Revolution and Man's Responsibility,* a failure to qualify, a certain flat-footed presumptuousness. It may sound a bit racy for a theological professor. They should remember that these were lectures delivered to a group of five hundred brash and presumptuous students. They were intended in part to spark discussion and disagreement, not to present a refined and finished position for an eternal record. I see no reason why, in the published version of the lectures, I should go through the manuscript adding qualifying adverbs and subtracting vivid adjectives. If the lectures were designed to evoke response, why should the book not serve the same purpose? If there are those who feel I overstate my case, let them overstate their response, and let us follow the argument, as Plato said, wherever it may lead.

Finally there are those who may dismiss this book as an ill-starred attempt to revive something called the "social gospel" which they had thought was safely embalmed. I am not the least bit embarrassed by this comparison. Who could be ashamed to be compared with Walter Rauschenbusch, one of the great theologians and prophets of American Christianity? Yet I would have to point out honestly that there are real differences between the ideas sketched out in this book and the perspective generally labeled "social gospel." The difference can probably be symbolized by the fact that the social gospel came before, and this book comes after, Karl Barth, Reinhold Niebuhr, and the enormous contribution of what has sometimes been called "dialectical" or neo-reformation theology.

We all stand today in the shadow of Karl Barth. That is why there is such an emphasis in this book on man's responding to God's holy initiative. Even the title of the book begins with what God is doing, with what man does forming the derivative element of the title. Those who have influenced my thinking include (besides Karl Barth) Dietrich Bonhoeffer, Gerhard von Rad, Hans Hoekendyjk, Paul Lehmann, and Richard Niebuhr. I have had the great privilege of knowing the last three of these personally, and I have studied under the last two. All of them represent a theological era which is far beyond both the original social gospel and its anxious conservative detractors.

Still there is nothing wrong with a "social" gospel, so long as it is both genuinely social and authentically gospel. Indeed it is hard to see how the biblical gospel can be anything else but social in the deepest sense of that term. I object to the designation only if it serves as a category by which the ideas expressed in this book can be tabbed and then discarded before they are examined. If they are to be rejected, let it be on their own merit or lack of it, not because they have been falsely tied to traditional stereotypes.

Finally let me thank the staff and students of the Baptist Student Movement who patiently sat through these perorations during those hot days at Green Lake, and the people of the Judson Press who kept after me for this manuscript when lesser souls would have given me up for an incorrigible procrastinator. I hope the book stimulates zealous discussion among us about where the God who disclosed himself in Jesus of Nazareth is continuing his revolutionary work today.

HARVEY COX

Roxbury, Mass.
May 25, 1965

chapter 1
GOD'S REVOLUTIONARY WORLD

IT IS TIME THAT WE CHRISTIANS MOVE OUR FOCUS FROM the renewal of church to the renewal of world. M. M. Thomas, one of the leaders of the ecumenical movement and a great Indian Christian, said recently that the World Council of Churches, since its inception in 1948, has been far too obsessed with discussions about the church. His criticism applies to all of us. We have talked about the unity of the church, the mission of the church, the renewal of the church. We have talked far too much about the church, but not enough about God's world. This does not mean that we must devise some kind of nonchurch Christianity, but it does mean that we can correct our ecclesiastical overemphasis. As D. T. Niles, another Asian Christian, once put it, if we want to speak with God, then we had better find out something about the world because that is the only subject in which God is interested. This book is about the renewal of the world, and our responsibility for it.

Let us take a look at the meaning of this world from a biblical perspective. Our starting point would be the opening words of the Bible: "In the beginning God created the heavens and the earth." We begin there because our thinking should start with what God has done and is doing in the world. Only then can we discover how through the church we respond to what he is calling us to be and to do in the world.

The New Testament uses several terms to refer to the world. It uses the word *kosmos* (orderly arrangement), for example, from which we get the words "cosmic," "cosmonaut," and even "cosmetic." It also uses the word *aiōn*, from which we have our word "eon," designating a long period of time. When we read through the New Testament, we are often confused by alternating negative and positive statements about the world. "Do not be conformed to the world," we hear; then we read on another page that "God so loved the world." We should be very careful, as we read the New Testament, to notice that one English word, "world," is used to translate two or three different Greek words. When the world is referred to positively, the word *kosmos* is most often used. When it is referred to negatively, either *aiōn* is used or an adjective such as "fallen" is placed before *kosmos*. The word *aiōn* could also be translated "world spirit" or "fallen age" rather than "world." The Bible has nothing against "the world."

When the Hebrew people talked about the "world,"

they didn't mean simply the stage on which the drama
of human enterprise is played out — not just the rocks
and hills. They meant the cast of this drama, too:

> The earth is the Lord's and the fulness thereof,
> the world and those who dwell therein. . . .

What the Hebrews had in mind here was not simply
a physical entity. They meant a "lived world," the
world of human decisions and dependencies, the inter-
locking spheres of hope and frustrations, the social
world, the cultural world; what we might call the human world. They meant the *kosmos*, insofar as it became the sphere of man's aspirations and man's meaning. This is the world as the Bible sees it.

Let me illustrate this meaning further from contemporary usage. We often talk about the "business
world" or the "world of entertainment," referring not
just to the physical properties of these worlds, but to
their human reality. Likewise, when we speak of "the
campus," we don't mean simply the green turf but
rather the human life which is lived in this community
called the campus. I think this comparison helps us to
understand what the Bible means when it says "world."
It means the entire constellation of all these interrelated
human worlds.

What does the Bible say about this world? I would
like to list four assertions the Bible makes about the
world.

*First assertion: The world is created, sustained, and
judged by God.* It is his creation. It belongs to him.
"The pillars of the earth are the Lord's," says Hannah
in 1 Samuel, "and on them has he set the world." We

should make clear at the outset that this is not a statement about the physical origin of the solar system. It is not something intended to rival some geological or astronomical theory about where the Milky Way or the planet Earth came from. Rather, this is a statement of the Hebrew community's faith that the world belongs to God, that he is the continuing source of our very life itself — of our common life — and that he stands as its ground, sustaining it and making it possible. It is a confession by the Hebrew people of the same thing that we mean when we sing "He's Got the Whole World in His Hands." It is a confession that all we have and all we are and all we can ever be comes to us from somewhere else, from someone else. It is a confession that there is no such thing as a self-made man. When Zampano in Federico Fellini's unforgettable film, *La Strada,* says, "All I want is to be left alone; I don't need anyone," he is denying the very basis of life. The breath that we breathe, the bodies that are ours, the very name that we bear, the language that we speak, all of these are given to us by others. There is no self-made man. We all stand in daily need of the God who is as near to us as the nearest thou, because it is through the nearest thou that God bestows life on us daily.

The creation story is also a confession that the world is good. God made it and saw that it was good — except for one thing: There were no women. So God finished making it good by creating a woman: "It is not good that the man should be alone." When we say that God created the world, we are affirming that it is good that he has placed us in a relationship of inter-dependency on one another as men and women, as human beings who can't get along without each other. Our first assertion, then, is that the world is created, sustained, and judged, and lies in the hands of God.

The second biblical assertion about the world is that the world is the object of God's love and concern. "God so loved the world that he gave his only son . . . not to condemn the world, but that the world might be saved through him." God loved the world, not the church. Jesus came and lived and taught and died in the world. He came into this human world of interdependency and reciprocity, a world characterized by human beings' need for each other. He became involved in this world, dependent on other human beings, subject to rejection, hatred, inattention, frustration. It is *this* world that God reconciled to himself. God was in Christ reconciling the *world* to himself, not the church. This world is the object of God's love and concern; God wants man to love this world, not to reject it. He wants man to have dominion over the world, to take care of it responsibly, to celebrate the astonishing fact that it is here, to thank God for it, to participate joyfully in it.

Let us look again at the story of God's creation of the world and his creation of Adam, "the man." It is hardly necessary to say that Adam was, of course, not the first Cro-Magnon who crawled up to the level of *Homo sapiens*. "Adam" is you and I, those whom God creates and to whom he assigns responsibility. God says to this Adam, in effect: "Have dominion over the world, tend the garden, cultivate it, be responsible in your care and concern for this world, love it, celebrate it."

He also tells Adam to name the animals. It is both fascinating and significant that God did not name the creatures himself. A name denotes meaning and purpose. God does not give names to the objects of our physical universe, to the things that we find around us. It is to man that God has assigned this responsibility. So God brought the giraffe, the pterodactyl, and the microorganism to Adam, for he wanted to see what man would name them. The Bible says that "whatever the man called every living creature, that was its name." God did not have any secret names he was getting ready to give these animals, which he put in the mind of man. He gave man the responsibility. It continues to be our responsibility to give meaning and significance to the things that we find in our universe. Nowadays we find a lot more of them than our forefathers did. We find whole world systems, whole microcosmic and macrocosmic systems that we have to name, and to which we have to give purpose. This naming is a much larger task, perhaps, than our forefathers had, but it is the same task — to love and to give significance and direction to the world in which we are placed. We are to make a joyful noise, to clap our hands, say the Psalmists, because we as men are given this world to love, to nourish, and to cultivate.

Another way to express the same idea is to say that for God the world is a life-and-death matter. He is willing to die for it, and our assignment is to have the same love for the world that he has. "As thou didst send me into the world," said Jesus, "so I have sent them into thy world." As God comes to the world, so does his church go to the world to love it, to be ultimately concerned about it in life-and-death terms. Our second assertion, then, is that the world is God's life-and-death concern, the object of his love and of his renewing activity.

The third assertion is that the world (by this I mean the political and secular world) is the sphere of God's liberating and renewing activity. The world is the theater of God's being with man. The God of the Bible, in rather sharp distinction to the other so-called gods and deities of the ancient Near East was characterized precisely by the fact that he worked in and through political events. He would not share his deity with the stars, nor the sun, nor the moon. These bodies were merely things that God had created, not divine beings. The God of the Hebrews was the God who revealed himself in the exodus, in the conquest, in the exile, in the defeat of the kingdom. He revealed himself in political events, in the liberation of the people from economic serfdom and political slavery, in the military conquest of the land, in the defeat at the hands of a world power. Thus he used political and military events to get the things done in history that he wanted done. He was perfectly willing to use people who denied him, people who had never heard about him, and even people who defied him, to do his work. The forty-fifth chapter of Isaiah illustrates how the biblical God uses those who deny him. Here God is depicted as speaking to Cyrus, the king of the Persians. Cyrus was certainly not a Christian, not even a Jew, but a pagan conqueror, a worshiper of false gods. So perhaps wherever the world "Cyrus" is used in the passage you might, to make it contemporary, substitute the name, Mao Tsetung or Castro.

> Thus says the Lord to his anointed, to Cyrus,
>   whose right hand I have grasped,
> to subdue nations before him
>   and ungird the loins of kings,
> to open doors before him
>   that gates may not be closed:
> ". . . I am the Lord, and there is no other,
>   besides me there is no God;
>   I gird you, though you do not know me,
> that men may know, from the rising of the sun
>   and from the west, that there is none beside me;
>   I am the Lord, and there is no other. . . ."

God used people who did not know him. He anointed them. The word "anoint" is the same word we use for "ordained." He set them aside and had them do his work. He used them, furthermore, through political events. The God of the Bible was and is a God who is only secondarily interested in nature. He is first and foremost interested in political events. The story of God's creating the heaven and the earth, the hills and the streams, came later in the development of the Hebrew faith than the first assertion that he was the God who "brought us out of Egypt, from the house of bondage." In order to read our Bibles correctly, we ought to read Exodus first and then Genesis, because this is the order in which the Hebrews came to their understandings. This primacy is very important, because when we speak about God's presence in the sacraments we must notice that we are not talking about the presence of God in some kind of natural element — in bread, or wine, or grape juice. We are talking about the way God makes himself present in an *action*, in the *breaking* and *distributing* of the good things of the earth, in making available to all men something to quench their thirst and to satisfy their hunger. This is where God is present, and we are immediately on the wrong track if we start by identifying God primarily with natural phenomena, whether it is sunsets or beautiful lakes.

God is first of all present in political events, in revolutions, upheavals, invasions, defeats. When the Bible speaks of God, it is almost always in political language. It talks about a covenant, which means a "treaty." It talks about judges, kings, and the Messiah — one who brought in a new kingdom, a kind of revolutionary. All these titles, unfortunately, have been falsely spiritualized and religionized over the years of Christian history. But, except very peripherally, there are *no* "religious words" used to describe God in the Old Testament. The word used for the "service of God" in the Old Testament is also used to refer to the service of a soldier or a citizen in the army of the king. Unfortunately this word has been translated as "worship," which has a cultic and spiritual significance for us that it did not have in the Hebrew. The other biblical term referring to worship really relates to a symbolic act of allegiance something like our military salute, by which a subject of the king or a soldier in the army symbolized his allegiance and willingness to obey. Unfortunately this word is also translated as "worship."

Perhaps it is our task as Christians in the twentieth century, at the end of what Bonhoeffer calls the "religious era" to begin now to despiritualize all of these words, to give them back their gritty, earthy, political significance. This, then, is the third assertion: It is the world, the political world and not the church, which is the arena of God's renewing and liberating activity. The church participates in this liberation only insofar as it participates in the world. To turn our back on the world is to turn our back on the place where God is at work.

The fourth assertion is simply a kind of logical conclusion of the first three: The world is the proper location of the Christian life. It is where the Christian is called to be a Christian. It is where his discipline and devotion, his defeats and victories occur. The world is the place of Adam's assignment, the place of Jesus' ministry, the place of the church's mission. The Gospel writers tell us that Jesus spent his time with people called the *Am ha-Aretz,* those beyond the pale of morality and law, including drunkards, winebibbers, and shady characters. He turned his back on the accepted moral and religious leaders of the day and spent his time in what we would call the seamy side of the world. Here were the people with whom and through whom he carried out his ministry. His career was climaxed in a clash with the urban power structures. He was executed on a public dump, and the sign over his gibbet was written in three languages. The crucifixion occurred at a crossroads of the world. This is where it *continues* to occur, where languages and cultures clash, where the urban power structures in their injustices are challenged, where people are willing to turn their backs on the accepted religious and moral standards of the day in order to stand with God in what he is doing for the world.

The world is a place into which Christians have been sent: "Go into all the world." Jesus says in his final prayer, "I do not pray that thou shouldst take them out of the world but that thou shouldst keep them from the evil one." The evil one is always tempting us to turn our back on the world, to take the "religious" way out, to preserve ourselves, to strive for our own sanctification at the expense of the renewal of the world. When Jesus prays that we not be taken out of the world, he means as Christians we have no special entrée to what is happening in the world. It means that we work alongside non-Christians and live with them, because this is the only way to be present in the world. We have no private entrance.

Let us sum up. God has the whole world; it is in his hands. This world, not the church, is the object of God's life-and-death concern. He works through the world, not just through the church, to accomplish his purposes. Later on we shall say something about the church, about how the church participates in God's activities in the world, but first of all we have to clear the stage of our obsessive talk about the church so that we can begin to talk about the world.

We can bring this a little closer to home if we can

take the word "campus" as one segment of this lived human world and say the things about it that we have said about the world at large. Instead of "world" and "church," let us substitute "campus" and "Baptist Student Center." It is not the Baptist Student Center, but the campus for which God has a life-and-death concern — which is the object of God's love. It is not the Baptist Student Center, but the campus which is the sphere of God's renewing activity. Those who would like to participate in God's renewing activity should realize that the only place to do it is on the campus, for this is the proper locus of the student Christian's life. It is into the campus that he is sent and it is there that he meets the One who is there already, anticipating his arrival and allowing the privilege of participating in his mission — mission which is first of all God's and only secondarily the student's.

Two dangers have crept into our thinking as Christians and have tended to distort the biblical understanding of the world:

1. The first, as we have just said, is that there is entirely too much talk about the church — the mission of the church, the nature of the church, the renewal of the church, and so on. This fault is present even in the Student Christian Movement, which unfortunately in the last fifteen or twenty years has become progressively more clericalized. In the "good old days" the student movement wasn't so interested in ecclesiastical talk. It is good that we are getting back to some of the "holy worldliness" which characterized those earlier days. The first task of the church is to discern the presence and

the activity of God in the world and to follow him there, where he *is*.

God has been doing things in the world in the past fifteen or twenty years, far in advance of the church. Professional baseball, and not the church in your community, took the first step integrating the races. We are very late in this whole business. We must run to catch up to what God is already doing in this world.

Those who were present on August 28, 1963, between the Washington Monument and the Lincoln Memorial for the March on Washington can testify to the quiet but firm determination of a large group of our citizens who will not wait any longer for the church to decide whether it wants to take the lead in integration. Eugene Carson Blake, of the United Presbyterian Church, was right when he said there:

> And it is partially because the churches of America have failed to put their own houses in order that 100 years after the Emancipation Proclamation, 175 years after the adoption of the Constitution, 173 years after the adoption of the Bill of Rights, the United States of America still faces a racial crisis.
>
> We do not, therefore, come to this Lincoln Memorial in any arrogant spirit of moral or spiritual superiority to "set the nation straight" or to judge or to denounce the American people in whole or in part.
>
> Rather we come — late, late we come — in the reconciling and repentant spirit in which Abraham Lincoln of Illinois once replied to a delegation of morally arrogant churchmen. He said, "Never say God is on our side, rather pray that we may be found on God's side." [1]

This is the situation in which we find ourselves as

[1] *New York Times*, August 29, 1963, p. 21.

Christians now — racing to catch up and once again be found on God's side — because he is way ahead of us. He is using forces and movements quite apart from the Christian church, as he has always done, to accomplish his purposes in the world.

2. The other way in which we have distorted the biblical picture of God's world is by an overspiritualization of the meaning of the Christian life. This is the most sinister distortion of the Bible abroad today. The spiritualizers always try to banish God from the earth and to distort the pictures of how he gets his work done in his world. Spiritualization is the characteristic heresy of the twentieth century, especially among American Protestants. The biblical faith has been transformed into a gaseous chimera.

The task of Christians in our generation is to restore the Old Testament earthliness and solidity to the wispy language of Christianity. This is not a new battle; it has been fought all through the years of Christian history, and not always with success. The language of traditional theology fails us at many points. If a Hebrew twenty-five hundred years ago had been asked to tell something about his God, it would never have occurred to him to say "omnipotent," "omnipresent," or other words which we have inherited from our theological tradition. His answer would have been specific and unpolished: "He is the God of Abraham, Isaac, and Jacob. He is the God who brought us up out of the house of bondage." This is a political god, a relational god, and yet also the god and father of our Lord Jesus Christ. He is no discarnate wraith. Our faith is centered on events as tangible as nails, as substantial as thorns, and as human as the cry of pain.

In fact, the Bible simply does not know any spiritual realm, any religious realm separate from the carnal realm. The spirit in the Bible is precisely that which enlivens and directs bodily activity. Very early in the Bible, God tips us off to his method of working in the world. He frees the captive people from economic and political bondage. He does not free these people to some kind of inner forbearance or of spiritual liberty; they *don't* say with Richard Lovelace,

> If I have freedom in my love,
> And in my soul am free,
> Angels alone, that soar above,
> Enjoy such liberty.[3]

No, he frees them to a new economic and political existence in the world; they are no longer slaves to Pharaoh. The biblical God recognizes no inner freedom apart from external conditions of freedom. He is not simply concerned with "nice feelings" between races, for example, but with the structural necessities which make racial reconciliation possible — integrated schools, open employment, unrestricted housing. These are the settings in which human beings once again become brothers. The world as God made it is an integrated world, but segregation of any sort is a rickety artifice made by man. Theologians need to engage not so much in demythologizing as in despiritualizing the Bible. The best way to do this is to stand with one foot in the Old Testament and one foot in the political struggles of our

[3] "To Althea, from Prison."

world today. From this dual standpoint, one can examine what God is saying to modern man in the New Testament. Any other position, I think, distorts what he is saying.

Of course, we have to add that the world as God makes it, as he gives it to us, and as he places us in it, is not the world as we have taken it from him. We have dislocated and distorted God's world. We created our own cardboard world in which we prefer to live rather than in God's world. God gave man and still gives him dominion over the forces of the world; but, instead of having dominion over the world, we decide to give the world dominion over us. Take, for example, money, political power, sex, work, play — all the things that go into this wonderful world that God has given us, the things he has given us to enjoy and to have in reciprocity with each other. We have made them our little tin masters and ourselves their slaves. Rather than utilizing these things as the God-given means of creating community between man and his fellowman, man and woman, labor and management, nation and nation, we have used them to beat down and to misuse those other human beings through whom God would come to us — the God who is as near to us as the nearest thou. We have rejected the world that God makes and that God gives us. We have fabricated our own little world around our family, our nation, our race, or our class. In so doing we deny the very principle of life as God makes it — interdependence — or we try as hard as we can to squeeze God into something called the "religious area" of life.

There is always one section of *Time* magazine each week devoted to religion. I am sure this is the last section that God reads, if in fact he reads *Time* magazine. God is much more interested in the world than he is in religion. Archbishop Temple once said that God is probably not interested in religion at all. Don't for a moment believe that religion is the sure road from man to God or even that it is the road from God to man. The great theological service performed by Karl Barth for our generation was his warning that religion is often the last battleground on which man fights *against* God and tries to make God something less than the sovereign of all of life.

God has created a world, and we have messed it up. God has given us a world, and we have refused it and made our own — but our own world is a phoney, ramshackle one and God's world is the real world. No matter how we try to avoid this real world that God is constantly creating and making anew, it is always breaking in on us, and sometimes God uses a Cyrus to do the breaking-in.

> Thus says the Lord to his anointed, to Cyrus,
>   whose right hand I have grasped, . . .
> to open doors before him
>   that gates may not be closed.
> ". . . I will break in pieces the doors of bronze
>   and cut asunder the bars of iron. . . ."

As children we have all seen the famous picture of Jesus standing outside the door and have been told by Sunday School teachers to notice that there was no knob on the outside of this door. The only way God can open it, we were told, is for us to open it from the inside. But, if we had read the forty-fifth chapter of Isaiah, we would recognize that when we don't want to open the door, God sometimes finds a Cyrus and smashes the door down. God is continuing to find Cyruses now to bash down the doors that we do not feel we are quite ready to open. He doesn't always wait for the church to be willing and ready. He finds a Cyrus so that, while we are satisfying ourselves with our flimsy caricature world, God is breaking in upon us with his real world again.

This breaking-in by God is what is happening in our present world revolutions. We must use the plural because there are several revolutions going on simultaneously, and it is sometimes very hard to separate them. There is an anticolonial revolution which has reached a fantastic speed and pace in the last decade. There is a scientific revolution in which man is once again assuming dominion over the earth and exercising the privilege of naming the animals. There is a revolution for racial freedom in which the people in this world who don't have white skin have determined they will no longer play second fiddle to the white minority. There is a peace revolution going on, and we find ourselves with an economy geared to a cold war. God is in all those revolutions.

There is a secular revolution going on, too — a secular revolution in which the dominance of ecclesiastical powers is being challenged, in which a real pluralism is emerging in America and the ancient stranglehold of feudal and aristocratic churches in Europe and in South

America is being broken down. God is in this revolution too, although it is harder to see him there. No doubt it is hard for us to concede that God works through secularization, the revolution against the remnants of religious world views. But he does. Jesus of Nazareth was the first person to challenge the unquestionable authority of the religious world view. The clue to all of Jesus' teachings, perhaps, is in his recurring words, "You have heard that it was said to men of old. . . . But I say to you. . . ." No inherited religious or moral teaching, regardless of its weight of ancestral authority, can now go unchallenged.

God is breaking the bar on the door of our rickety shack, the creation which we put up in the face of his creation. He is coming in to us. He is renewing and re-creating his world, and he wants us to be a part of his reconstructing activity. This is the call of evangelism. This is the invitation to be a Christian, to come from where we are and to be a part of what God is doing in this world. Man is once again being given his dominion over the created order. We are once again discovering our interdependence. Women, colored peoples, colonies, all the persons we have used as objects are asserting now that they too have dignity and personhood. Equally significant is the fact that in our own nation religious escapism is disappearing. William Stringfellow on the first page of his book, *A Private and Public Faith*, says that the religious revival in America is dead and that this is the best thing that could have happened to the gospel of Jesus Christ. Stringfellow is right. Since God works in the world, and religion is often a way of escaping from the world, the demise of the "religious revival" is in fact a *very* good thing.

There may be some who will be troubled by these statements. Is this reaction really very new? Who was it about whom the writer of the Acts said, "These men who have turned the world upside down have come here also"? They weren't Communists. Who were they? Paul L. Stagg writes about rapid social change in Latin America in this way: "Constructive change is not a threat to order or stability, except to an *unjust* order, but rather a prelude to an authentic order. God's order (the peace of justice) is not on this side of change, but on the other side. The more fixed and inflexible a society becomes the more dehumanized it becomes." Continuing, he quotes from Richard Shaull, who has been working for twenty years with the students of South America as a missionary: "Change is the way the God of justice shatters an unjust order and opens up the way of God's will for justice." [8] Not only is change willed by God, but it is God who brings about change. He is on the move, and if we want to be related to him we must be on the move also.

God's activity in the world today is a call to us to become the kind of Christians whose witness and discipline are relevant to what he is doing in our century. To respond to this call requires discipline. It has been accurately reported that we as free churchmen have lost the sense of discipline. But the discipline we must recover in order to participate in God's reconstruction of

[8] "Secular Revolt Against the Ecclesiastical System," *Missions*, November, 1963, p. 18.

the world is different from the discipline our grand-fathers had. Arthur Koestler says that what we need today is a mixture of the saint and the revolutionary. What he is calling for is a blend of the humility and passion of the classical saint with the political realism and the "engagement" of the revolutionary.

It is curious, isn't it, that so much of our best biblical and other Christian literature has been written behind bars. Why do you suppose that is? Is it because Christians are called to be God's avant-garde, *already* living in the new era, *already* living in the kingdom of justice, brotherhood, and peace that God is bringing in? This citizenship of the future kingdom as it already becomes present often involves us in conflict with the custodians of the past. The passage from Isaiah which I have quoted was obviously written by a prophet in captivity. Paul's epistle to the Philippians was written in a jail. More recently another saint-revolutionary has written not from a Babylonian or Philippian jail, but from a Birmingham jail and his words say something about the call of Christians to catch up with God in what he is doing in his world. Writes Martin Luther King:

There was a time when the church was very powerful — in the time when the early Christians rejoiced at being deemed worthy to suffer for what they believed. In those days the church was not merely a thermometer that recorded the ideas and principles of popular opinion; it was a thermostat that transformed the mores of society. Whenever the early Christians entered a town the power structure immediately sought to convict them for being "disturbers of the peace" and "outside agitators." But the Christians pressed on, in the conviction that they were "a colony of heaven" called to obey God rather than man. . . . But the judgment of God is upon the church as never before.[4]

In Fellini's film, *La Strada*, the clown tells the girl Gelsomina to stay with the unlovable Zampano. "If you don't love him and stay with him," he asks, "who else will?" This is a parable of our calling in God's revolutionary world. We are called to love this world and "stay with it," to take upon our shoulders the responsibility for its reconstruction and renewal. This is the assignment that God has given us, and he will give us the strength to fulfill it.

[4] *The Christian Century*, June 12, 1963, p. 772. Copyright 1963 by the Christian Century Foundation. Reprinted by permission.

chapter 2

SIN:
MAN'S BETRAYAL
OF HIS MANHOOD

Gᴏᴅ ʜᴀꜱ ɢɪᴠᴇɴ ᴍᴀɴ ᴀ ᴛʜʀɪʟʟɪɴɢ ʀᴇꜱᴘᴏɴꜱɪʙɪʟɪᴛʏ ꜰᴏʀ this world. But man has not fulfilled his assignment. God has placed the tiller of history in man's hand, but man has gone to his hammock and let the winds and tides sweep his ship along. Man has done things he ought not to have done, but even more importantly he has not done those things he ought to have done. He has refused to live up to the full stature of his manhood and has abdicated his crucial place in the scheme of things. This is what biblical tradition has called "sin."

Can we make any sense whatever out of the traditional idea of sin today? I would suggest that the term in our contemporary vocabulary which comes closest

---

This chapter is adapted from an article, "Apathy, Abdication, and Acedia," originally published in the magazine, *Renewal*, January-February, 1965, pp. 18-20.

to what the Bible means by sin is "apathy," or perhaps "sloth." Admittedly, trying to understand modern apathy in the light of the notion of sin is no easy task, but we must make the attempt, for, unless we include some understanding of the place of man's sin in a discussion of mission, we shall have overlooked a crucial factor. And, unless we come to some viable understanding of the apathy which warps and paralyzes us today, we shall misunderstand the character of the modern world.

Sin is not a popular theological subject today and when it comes to teaching us what it is really all about, our two best instructors in recent years have not been theologians, but Hannah Arendt and James Baldwin. Arendt's portrait of Adolf Eichmann, *Eichmann in Jerusalem,* subtitled "A Study in the Banality of Evil," despite some justifiable criticisms made of it, remains a graphic portrayal of sin in the twentieth century — monstrous crimes perpetrated by insipid sad-sacks. It terrifies us because Eichmann is so overpoweringly ordinary, so like us. As his featureless face gradually takes form in Arendt's pages, he is disclosed as the kind of spectacle-polishing milquetoast with whom we would be bored after ten minutes if we had to sit next to him on a commuter train. Yet it is Eichmann's vapid triteness which reflects our own sin. Incapable of Luciferian evil, we could all commit genocide just by getting to work on time and keeping our noses clean.

If Arendt dismantles our prevailing images of sin by introducing us to the dolt-as-deathmonger, Baldwin performs the same service inversely by seeing in the Negro militant the saint-as-revolutionary. Others have used such an image before, especially Arthur Koestler and Ignazio Silone. But they were both too European in their mentality to speak to many Americans. Baldwin gets to us because he opens our eyes to the saints among us. And they are not the otherworldly, self-effacing saints of the religious bookstores but angry hotheads, impetuous activists impatiently pursuing social change and spiritual wholeness. In providing us with a new model of religious obedience, Baldwin has also exposed the criminal sinfulness of our law-abiding complacency and inactivity.

The sharpened awareness of sin which Baldwin and Arendt have brought us catches Christian theologians at an embarrassing time. The truth is that the ideas of sin with which we are now working are probably more Greek than biblical, and not even very good Greek at that. The word "sin" itself has lurid, titillating, and tempting overtones. It suggests sentimentality and cultural repressions thinly coated with pictures of Adam and Eve and a superbly phallic serpent.

Admittedly theologians have been working for some years now to repair the damages done to Christian theology by the uncritical importation of Greek categories. Work is proceeding apace on historical theologies and secular ethics. God has *almost* become a Hebrew again. But in the meantime our images of man remain largely Greek, or more precisely, Promethean.

The confused process of thought goes as follows: Pride is rightly seen as the basic element of man's sin; but then pride is mistakenly identified with rebelliousness and man-the-sinner is wrongly pictured as the fist-shaking, contemptuous insurrectionary. He is seen as the creature who "doesn't know his place," who storms the heavens with such audacity that God must constantly summon the host to quell the revolt. This basically Greek image, larded here and there with the cautionary warnings of bourgeois culture, has persisted in diverting our attention from the main thrust of the Bible for centuries. The result in western literature has been a none-too-secret admiration for man as the heroic sinner. Projected mythologically we find Lucifer and Satan, whether in Goethe or in Milton, far more interesting than anyone else. While officially condemning them to flames, we secretly admire them. This distorted image of the sinner-as-rebel has become so deeply lodged in the western mentality that in our own day Emil Brunner (*Man in Revolt*) and Albert Camus (*The Rebel*) both agree that the rebellious human spirit must, by definition, be anti-Christian. Needless to say the former condemns such a spirit while the latter celebrates it.

We need to make a whole new start in reformulating a biblical doctrine of sin which makes sense of a modern world, with its dutifully compliant Eichmanns and its lawbreaking Martin Luther Kings, and is at the same time closer to the Bible than the one we have now.

Let us suggest that the ancient and venerable term *sloth* may help us in this undertaking. Sloth means being *less* than, not more than, man. Sloth means the determined or lackadaisical refusal to live up to one's essential humanity. It is the torpid unwillingness to revel in the delights or to share in the responsibilities of being fully human. It means to decline a full share of that characteristic life-with-life which *is* human existence in the world.

"Sloth" is the English word we use to translate the Latin word *acedia,* which is derived in turn from the Greek words "not caring" (*a* — not; *kedos* — care). The Church Fathers listed sloth (along with pride, covetousness, lust, anger, gluttony, and envy) as one of the seven deadly, or capital sins. Calvin emphasized sloth heavily, but the later Calvinist theologians associated it too closely with the bourgeois-capitalist vice of laziness or lack of ambition. Theologians have generally conceded that both pride and sloth played an important role in man's sin, that the two are in some sense inextricable. Why then has pride, seen almost always as rebellion, been so over-emphasized while sloth (*acedia*) has been nearly forgotten?

One reason is that we have located the fall of man too narrowly in the forbidden fruit fable in Genesis. "In Adam's fall we sinned all." And so we did, or do; but modern biblical scholars indicate that the *whole* first section of Genesis, not just the Adam and Eve story, was intended to illuminate man's fractured relationship to the creation. Thus the stories of Cain and Abel, of Noah and the Ark, and of the Tower of Babel are just as important as the Garden of Eden story in symbolizing the character of man's sin. They all concern the ways in which man abdicates his assignment of living in brotherly reciprocity with his fellow man and with the natural order. He is always looking for a way out. Instead of faithfully naming the creatures whom God entrusts to him, cultivating the garden of the earth and enjoying its fruits, exercising dominion over the beasts, and living in reciprocity with his fellow man, he sells out.

The first thing he does is to let one of the animals tell him what to do. He surrenders his position of privilege and responsibility. From then on there is nothing but trouble. Pride and sloth then work in tandem to disfigure the world. Thus to read the story of the fall entirely in terms of defiant pride is to rely on Sophocles rather than the Genesis account, the only difference being that, for the Greeks, King Oedipus was in some strange way fulfilling his destiny by defying fate while, for the Bible, Adam was frittering away his destiny.

In Adam, the man who at first will not and then cannot be man, the Bible sees all men. But with the coming of the Second Adam, Christ, that situation changes. Here was a man who would be and was a full man. In him the whole range of human responsibility is fully taken up again. He exercises the full prerogatives of manhood. He lives in vigorous reciprocity with thieves, priests, prostitutes, and little children. In the stories that Jesus spins, one of the most frequent characters is the steward, the man who has the responsibility and exercises the power assigned to him by the master. The cautious or irresponsible steward, the one who hides his money in the earth or beats the servants in the master's absence, reaps the rebuke of Jesus. The Apostle Paul also sees the life that God makes possible for man as that of an heir who, putting childhood dependencies firmly behind him, assumes the duties of an adult. *It is thus quite evident that images of timidity, abdication, and irresponsibility should figure just as prominently in a biblical doctrine of sin as do images of rebellion.* Why then has our theological tradition concerned itself so obsessively with insubordination as the chief expression of sin?

Part of the answer can be given in the single word, *politics.* Theologies always develop within a particular political context. There is a political, or perhaps an ideological factor which explains in part why images of protest and revolt became so central in the Christian doctrine of sin. With the conversion of Constantine, Christianity became the ruling ideology of Europe. As such, one of its main functions was to provide the symbolic confirmation of imperial authority and thus to assure the maintenance of social order. It did so with noteworthy success for more than a thousand years of relatively unified western European "Christian" civilization. It did so by de-emphasizing sloth and accentuating pride as the worst form of sinfulness. Pride, of course, was equated with insubordination.

When the Reformation came, the magisterial reformers — Luther, Calvin, and the Anglicans — largely retained this emphasis. Since they had to rely so heavily on state power for carrying through their programs, they necessarily preserved the dominant image of sinful man as disobedient, fractious, and insubordinate. There can be little doubt that the opposition these reformers experienced from the more radical reformers — Muenzer, Servetus, the Levellers — encouraged the *identification of piety with passivity* in their own minds.

By the nineteenth century the merging of faith and docility had become so axiomatic that Kierkegaard, Marx, and Nietzsche all had to become enemies of Christendom to make themselves heard. Each was condemned by the church, but each was right in his own way. Kierkegaard taught that the only real sin was "the despairing refusal to be one's self"; Marx railed rightly against people who saw society as an eternal "given" rather than as something for which man himself is responsible. Nietzsche saw correctly that a vampire God who will not allow man to be a creator must be killed, and gladly performed that act of deicide himself. Each represents repentance from the sin of sloth at a different level. For Kierkegaard, and for those contemporary existentialists who are most influenced by him, the individual must choose his own identity and not allow himself to be named by the images and expectations others inflict upon him. For Marx, man had to discard his superstitious reverence for unjust social structures before he could begin to change them. Nietzsche hoped for a new man beyond the bourgeois clod of the nineteenth century, a man who would have the courage to shape the very symbols and meanings by which he would live in the world.

The sin against which these three nineteenth-century prophets preached is what classical theologians once called *acedia,* sloth.

Sloth is one of the seven "deadly," or more correctly, "capital" sins. This doesn't just mean it is quantitatively worse, but that it is a "source sin," the kind of structural derangement from which other sins arise. As Roman

Catholic theologian Josef Pieper remarks, sloth does not mean mere idleness, as though hyperthyroid activism were its antidote; rather it means that man "renounces the claim implicit in his human dignity." [1] In medieval terms this means that the slothful man does not will his own being, does not wish to be what he fundamentally and really is. This is why sloth is such a dangerously fertile sin. It tempts man to other expressions of inhumanity. It leads toward what we might today call estrangement.

God through history summons man to affirm and celebrate what God wants him to be: Man, with all that implies. As Kierkegaard, Marx, and Nietzsche saw, to be a man involves personal, social, and cultural initiative and responsibility. It means accepting the terrifying duty of deciding *who I will be* rather than merely introjecting stereotypes that others assign to me. It means opening my eyes to the way power is distributed and wielded in a society and assuming a full measure of pain and temptation that goes with wielding it. It means defying any image of life which discourages criticism or undercuts human creativity. Metaphors which are allowed to become metaphysical become monsters. To be a man means to care for and name the fellow-man Eve, and with her to have dominion over the earth; to name and care for the creature whom God places in the human world of freedom. To weasel out of any of these privileges is to commit the sin of *acedia*, to relapse into sloth.

[1] Josef Pieper, *Leisure, the Basis of Culture* (New York: Pantheon Books, 1952), p. 38.

All this suggests that apathy is the key form of sin in today's world. Apathy is one of the words used to define *acedia.* For Adam and Eve, apathy meant letting a snake tell them what to do. It meant abdicating what theologians have called the *gubernatio mundi,* the exercise of dominion and control over the world. For us it means allowing others to dictate the identities with which we live out our lives. Sartre's portrait of Jean Genet in *Saint Genet* depicts a man whose view of himself is totally dictated by the mean lusts and foul passions projected on him by others. The Jew, the Negro, the homosexual, and the beatnik in our society have sometimes been forced to enact some of these roles for us. But in projecting our secret fears and fantasies onto them we both impoverish ourselves and prostitute them. Man is that creature who is created and called by God to shape and enact his own destiny. Whenever he relinquishes that privilege to someone else, he ceases to be a man. It is precisely that Negro who takes off the Sambo costume, who stops playing the humiliating role whites have pasted together for him who thus affirms the promise of the New Adam. His decision to be himself is an act of repentance from sloth.

But apathy is also, and perhaps mainly, a political trespass. It takes the form of hiding behind a specialty, a lack of knowledge, a fear of involvement, but these devices become rationalizations for not assuming one's share in the responsible use of power in the world. Man's existence is by its very nature life with and for the fellow man. This makes it essentially political. The apathetic avoidance of politics is the sophisticated way in which we, like Cain, club our brothers to death. We abdicate our assignment as stewards, becoming what C. Wright Mills once called "inactionaries." From the slum Negro who doesn't vote or picket to the MIT scientist who lets Washington decide what shall be done with the weapons systems he is designing, to slough off the political life is to fall into the deadly sin of *acedia*, from which all sorts of lesser venial sins sprout and grow.

We must be careful today with all of our emphasis on the servant role of the church not to give the impression that the call of the gospel is to plebian servility. It is a call to adult stewardship, to originality, inventiveness, and the governance of the world. Let's not allow any snake to tell us what to do.

chapter 3

THE GOSPEL: GOD'S WORD FOR HIS WORLD

We LIVE IN THE TIME OF THE INVALIDATION OF THE Christian gospel by Christians themselves. We have managed to prove to most of the world's people that we don't really mean what we say. Under these circumstances, if we are to live in a world in which God *is* still alive and active despite us, we must begin by finding out *why* many people believe a self-invalidation of Christianity is taking place.

The truth is that we cannot understand today's world within the categories we received from our forefathers. The dimensions of the situation we are facing now in the United States and in the world are too new and shattering. The great fact is revolution, and we Christians simply don't know how to live with and in a revolution. It is reported that during the initial stages of Castro's movement, before he came into power and even for a short time thereafter, there were a number of Cuban Baptists in high positions in his movement. But, when they found a real revolution on their hands and wanted to make a Christian witness and contribution within a revolutionary situation, they were totally baffled. Most of them had to withdraw, go back to Oriente province, and turn over the running of this revolution to the Communists who at least seemed to know what they were doing. These Cuban Christians lacked the kind of theology of the world that we have to begin to develop; perhaps if they had not retreated, the story in Cuba might have been different.

This all becomes very important when we ask ourselves what we mean by "the Gospel" or by "the Word." We Christians have been a very talkative people, talkative to the point of verbosity, so it is understandable that we have misconstrued what the Word really is. When we look through the Bible, however, to discover what it says about the Word (*Dabar* in the Old Testament or *Logos* in the New Testament), then our whole understanding about words and talk is suddenly called into question. God's Word is *not* talk; God's Word is *action*, and this fact is very confusing to us.

When God talks, something happens. He *does* something. He speaks and the world is created. His Word brings light to the darkness. His Word judges, heals, cuts asunder. God's Word in the Bible is, in fact, not phrases and syllables, but ultimately it is hands and feet. In the final analysis God's Word for man is Jesus of Nazareth. He *is* God's Word. The writer of Hebrews puts it this way:

> In many and various ways God spoke of old to our fathers by
> the prophets; but in these last days he has spoken to us by a
> Son whom he appointed the heir of all things, through whom
> also he created the world.

So God has his own way of speaking to man and it is in
the language of events — a battle, an exile, a conquest,
a defeat, a captivity. He speaks through political in-
trigues and military campaigns, social upheavals and
revolutions. He also speaks in a still small voice such as
Elijah heard. This kind of speaking is the stuff of history. The history of God's people is the Old Testament,
and through their history God speaks to us today.

Whenever God turns to man, it is through his Word.
Through the Word, the first chapter of John tells us, the
world was created and finally this Word became flesh.
God's Word became an event, living among us, dying in
the tissue of time. Still, however, we might ask whether
this is really what we mean by God's Word, for it is not
what we ordinarily mean by "words" when we talk to
each other. It is not just talk.

What is it then? Why does the Bible refer to "the
Word"? Specifically, why does it use the terminology
of speech and hearing to refer to the way God addresses
man? Why does it only rarely use images of seeing,
touching, smelling, or some other form of perception?
I think there is a good reason for using speaking and
hearing as a symbol of the relationship between God
and man: Hearing necessitates involvement. I can
watch something from a distance totally uninvolved,
merely an observer. When someone *calls* me, however,
the word accosts me, arrests me, and demands a re-

sponse. Even if I refuse to respond, this refusal is itself a kind of response. I have to acknowledge in one way or another that I am spoken to, and such is always the relationship of God to man.

God's Word to man, by its very nature, cannot be ignored. It comes in such a way that I must answer it or refuse to answer it. God's Word, says the Bible, never returns to him void; it always elicits some response. If we think that God has spoken to us and that we have been able simply to ignore his voice, then it hasn't been God speaking at all. If, however, we have been accosted and challenged and our lives have been changed by some event that has come to us, then God may very well have been speaking to us through this event, even though we did not recognize him.

The Bible is full of incidents in which God spoke to man but man was unable to recognize God's voice in that event. For example, there were those people in Matthew 25 who asked: "Lord, when did we see thee hungry and feed thee, or thirsty and give thee drink? And when did we see thee a stranger and welcome thee or naked and clothe thee? And when did we see thee sick or in prison and visit thee?" And Jesus replied: "As you did it to one of the least of these my brethren, you did it to me." Thus he pointed out that God had been addressing them through an event, unrecognized. Then there were the disciples on the Emmaus road who did not know their companion was Jesus until he sat down with them to break bread. God always acts in this way. His Word is a deed, a life lived. And our response to God is also not simply verbal; it is a life lived in its totality — not just a fraction thereof, for that would be a caricature.

Jesus of Nazareth is God's Word to man. In him we find perhaps the only known person in whom word and deed always went together, for Jesus was as good as his word. He said, "I am the way, and the truth, and the life." In Jesus there was none of the schism between saying and doing which is in every one of us. As Rudolf Bultmann, the German theologian, pointed out, whatever Jesus says is a doing and whatever he does is a speaking, for his actions speak and his words act. So God has no wordy sermon for man, no choice aphorisms or religious maxims; he has but one Word, a life lived, Jesus of Nazareth. This is what we mean when we speak about the Word of God.

What is the *content* of this Word? There is one word which in a way sums up the entire content of what God says to us in Jesus of Nazareth and that is the old Hebrew term *shalom*. This is one of the most common greetings exchanged by the Jewish people, both in Old Testament days and in modern Israel. It is rich in overtones and in depth. Throughout the centuries of torture and hardship, through all the years of the whip and the torch that we as Christians have applied to the Jews, they have continued to greet each other and take leave with the word *shalom*. Mothers separated from their children and sent to Nazi concentration camps for medical experiments whispered as the last word to their little ones, "*Shalom!*" Segments of families reunited in Haifa or Tel Aviv after the war looked at each other, then broke the silence with "*Shalom!*"

We usually translate this word as "peace," but this rendering is quite inadequate. To the ancient Hebrew the word *shalom* meant a condition of personal and corporate life broader than the absence of armed conflict which our word "peace" designates, and broader also than the more recent watery soup of "peace of mind" or "peace of soul." It is nothing so individualistic, nothing so immaterial or shallowly spiritual. *Shalom* is a positive condition of peace, joy, human reciprocity, social harmony, exalted justice. It signifies abundance, good health, neighborliness. For the Hebrews, *shalom* was something suffusing the whole community life; it was dancing in the streets and clapping one's hands.

But *shalom* was something only God could provide, for it *is the character of the New Era that the Messiah brings*. He is the *Shalom* Bringer, the Prince of *Shalom*. Here is the description of the new kingdom as it appears in the book of Isaiah:

> For behold, I create new heavens
> and a new earth;
> and the former things shall not be remembered
> or come into mind. . . .
> [Men] shall build houses and inhabit them;
> they shall plant vineyards and eat their fruit.
> They shall not build and another inhabit;
> they shall not plant and another eat;
> for like the days of a tree shall the days of my people be,
> and my chosen shall long enjoy the work of their hands.
> They shall not labor in vain,
> or bear children for calamity. . . .

This is *shalom*. It is not simply the cessation of conflict; it is something positive. When the prophet Micah describes it as every man sitting "under his vine and under his fig tree," the prophet Zechariah goes even further and describes it this way: "In that day, says the Lord of hosts, every one of you will invite his neighbor under his vine and under his fig tree." In the distinction between the words of these two prophets is the difference between mere peace and *shalom*. *Shalom* is the exclusive content of the New Era. It is the character of the kingdom of God — the new regime of the Messiah. It is love, joy, and peace.

We don't have to turn only to the Old Testament prophets to find the idea of *shalom*. Let's turn to a modern prophet, to a few of the words uttered at Washington on August 28, 1963, by Martin Luther King before 200,000 persons as he describes his "dream":

> I say unto you today, my friends, that in spite of the difficulties and frustrations of the moment I still have a dream. It is a dream deeply rooted in the American dream. . . .
>
> I have a dream that one day on the red hills of Georgia the sons of former slaves and the sons of former slaveowners will be able to sit down together at the table of brotherhood.
>
> I have a dream that one day even the state of Mississippi, a desert state sweltering with the heat of injustice and oppression, will be transformed into an oasis of freedom and justice.
>
> I have a dream that my four little children will one day live in a nation where they will not be judged by the color of their skin, but by the content of their character.[1]

This statement stands in a long tradition of prophets who had dreams. There was Isaiah, whose words should be read as a promise:

[1] *The SCLC Story* (Atlanta: Southern Christian Leadership Conference, 1964), p. 51.

The people who walked in darkness
    have seen a great light;
those who dwelt in a land of deep darkness,
    on them has light shined.
Thou hast multiplied the nation,
    thou hast increased its joy. . . .
For to us a child is born,
    to us a son is given;
and the government will be upon his shoulder,
    and his name will be called
"Wonderful Counselor, Mighty God,
    Everlasting Father, Prince of *Shalom.*"
Of the increase of his government and of *shalom*
    there will be no end. . . .

This theme occurs often in the Old Testament. God told the sons of Aaron that every time they blessed Israel they should say: "The Lord bless you and keep you: The Lord make his face to shine upon you, and be gracious to you: The Lord lift up his countenance upon you, and give you *shalom.*"

The idea of *shalom* is also the opening chord struck in the New Testament.[2] Visualize the scene: Shepherds on a cold hillside, on a miserable night, crouched around the fires, blowing on their hands. Suddenly an angel appears and says a word which was laden with content for every Jew: "Glory to God in the highest, and on earth *shalom* among men with whom he is pleased!" Throughout the New Testament the concept appears time and time again. Jesus says: "*Shalom* I leave with you; my *shalom* I give to you; not as the world gives do I give to you." Paul begins all his let-

---

[2] The word used in the earliest available New Testament texts is the Greek *eirene* (peace) which this author interprets as representing *shalom.*

ters with warm greeting, and these invariably include some words like "Grace be to you and *shalom* from God the Father and from our Lord Jesus Christ."

Jesus is the *shalom* bringer, and the church is a people that lives and demonstrates the *shalom* of God. But, to understand what the church is for the world, we have to look at *shalom* and see what its component elements are. We will list three.

1. The first element of *shalom* is RECONCILIATION. Whatever else the church may be, it is a community which demonstrates and works for reconciliation. It helps bring about God's *shalom*. In 2 Corinthians 5: 17-18 Paul says: "Therefore, if any one is in Christ, he is a new creation; the old has passed away, behold, the new has come. All this is from God, who through Christ reconciled us to himself and gave us the ministry of reconciliation." In the next verse we find the connection between our chapter on "God's Revolutionary World" and the present discussion on "God's Word for His World." It is the *shalom* of God: "God was in Christ reconciling the world to himself." Continuing, Paul says that we are ambassadors for Christ, who has entrusted us with the ministry of this reconciliation; God makes his appeal through us. This is the reconciliation of God.

This reconciliation is also described in Ephesians 2: 14-15, where Paul says in so many words, "He is our peace *[shalom]* who . . . has broken down the dividing wall of hostility . . . that he might create in himself one new man in place of the two." We must examine the wall of hostility which Paul said was broken down in Jesus of Nazareth. What wall was it? For Paul it was the wall between the Jews and the Gentiles. If we think we have a segregation problem, we should examine the problem he had in the relationship between the Jews and the Gentiles. If we think the chasm between Russians and Americans is deep, then we should look at the chasm Paul was describing. All of the factors which divide us today were concentrated in this single division between the Jew and the Gentile; and, for Paul, when this wall was broken down, all barriers were gone.

What kind of barrier was this wall?

First of all it was a *religious* barrier. The Jews were those who had the covenant of God, and all the rest were outside the law, outside the promises. These were the religious people, and those were the nonreligious people. Second, it was a *racial* barrier (if indeed we can make any sense of the word "race" any more), the Jew and the non-Jew. Third, it was a *cultural* barrier. The Jews were those who maintained the Commandments, who carefully followed the precepts of the law, the observance of the Sabbath, and all the things which high morality required. They were recognized all over the Roman Empire as the representatives of the highest kind of morality. And, finally, it was a *political* barrier. The Jews were a captive nation, occupied by a Gentile army. More than one Roman soldier walking the streets of Jerusalem those days may have seen scrawled on the wall the equivalent of: "Roman, go home!"

In the face of this complex barrier between Jews

and non-Jews, what Paul says is that Jesus of Nazareth is man's *shalom*. Jesus hasn't simply desegregated us; he has brought us together into a community with all the rich overtones of *shalom*. It is not just a community in which every man can sit under his own fig tree and have the opportunity for a job, a house, or an education. *Shalom* is more than that. It is the kingdom in which every man invites his neighbor to come and sit under his fig tree. Jesus Christ is our *shalom* who has broken down the walls of hostility between men, who has made of the two one.

One could view the whole life of Jesus from first to last as a single continuing exploit in breaking down the walls that separate the people. The life of Jesus was a constant series of risky exploits, jumping over and short-circuiting the barriers which men erect between themselves. He broke down the walls between Jews and non-Jews, between the self-righteous Pharisees and the morally cynical publicans. His whole career presents a staggering series of calculated attempts to destroy the fictions that separate people from one another. Pursuing this indiscreet purpose, he shattered social conventions, trespassed on moral codes, and defied religious tradition. He simply refused to allow racial, class, or religious demarcations to hamper his movement, insisting that somehow in his own person all of these things were now abolished. He was the representation, the beginning of the regime of *shalom*. His execution is a grisly but vivid recapitulation of his whole life. He was helped by a black man to the hill where he was tortured to death along with criminals after being victimized by a kangaroo court of both Jews and Romans. The sign over his cross was written in three languages. So, in his death as in his life, Jesus of Nazareth — God's Word for us, God's *shalom* — is the center of reconciliation. The crucifixion was not a segregated event.

In the light of the crucifixion, it is very important for us to see what Jesus meant when he spoke of his "cup." "Remove this cup from me," he once prayed, "nevertheless not my will, but thine, be done." When he used the word "cup" he was talking about his *cross*. This understanding is desperately important when we discuss the so-called "sacraments" because, when Jesus invites us to partake of his cup, he is not inviting us to take a little sip of grape juice; he is inviting us to participate in wall-breaking, in living and dying as a representative of God's *shalom*. This is one of the points where our "despiritualization" must be relentless. To come to the table of the Lord, to participate in his broken body and in his shed blood is more than to munch white bread or drink grape juice. The apostle Paul, in the next section of 1 Corinthians after his description of the communion service, says: "Anyone who eats and drinks without discerning the body eats and drinks judgment on himself." God's Word to man in Jesus of Nazareth is *shalom* — reconciliation.

2. The next word we see as a constituent of God's *shalom* is FREEDOM. Jesus Christ is the one who frees us, the Bible keeps saying. He is the one who makes us free. This idea is hard for us to understand today because we believe that, if anybody can make us free from anything, it is we ourselves. How, then, can we

say that God in Jesus of Nazareth has made us free? What's this freedom all about?

Freedom, in the Bible, is first of all freedom for maturity. The opposite of bondage, as the Bible sees it, is not independence but responsibility. Freedom is the willingness to exercise responsible power and control over the things which normally dominate us. The Bible talks about our liberation *from* and *for, from* bondage and *for* service. It says we are freed *from* the principalities and powers and *for* our fellowmen. Let us look for a moment at these principalities and powers, for they disturb and bother modern readers of the Bible. We don't believe in principalities and powers, because we identify them with demons, spooks, and goblins. But we can break through this language barrier. When Jesus approaches someone who is sick of what we might call schizophrenia and says the person is "possessed of a demon," it is perfectly natural that he should speak this way. If Jesus was fully human like you and me, why should we expect him in the first century A.D. to have some kind of occult access to explanations that have only been discovered in this twentieth century? How would we feel if we read the Gospel of Mark and it described Jesus as saying of someone who is ill: "This man appears to be suffering from a case of schizophrenia or a character neurosis"? We would rightly ask whether this was really a first-century document. So let's understand that Jesus, like ourselves, thought and operated within the frames of reference of his day.

What Jesus was talking about, these principalities and

powers, these forces which pervert and distort, are still here today. We give them different names, but they are still among us. Not too long ago we smiled just a bit contemptuously at people who talked about *supra*human or *sub*human forces. Some things have happened, however, in western history in the past fifty years that have made us a little less sneering about the reality of such forces. We have only to mention two names to suggest the present intellectual respectability of speaking about the suprahuman and the subhuman — the names of Karl Marx and Sigmund Freud, two men who shook us out of our rational complacency, our intellectual arrogance. Freud showed us that there are subhuman forces below the level of conscious human personality which can pervert and distort life. Marx demonstrated that beyond our own individual decision-making there are unrecognized economic and political forces, class pressures, and historical currents which shape our decisions and hold us in bondage.

Let us not think, therefore, that when the New Testament talks about "principalities and powers" it is a document that we can simply dispose of as not speaking the language of the day. It is talking about forces that we still have. Today we call them blood, or class, or statistical probability; only the names are changed. Perhaps all of these forces — this entire range of symbols denoting the control of man's life by something other than man — can be called fate.

Fate is that over which man has no control, that in terms of which he is unfree and in bondage. Fate includes everything that serves to remove either freedom or responsibility from man's shoulders. We have all heard people blaming fate for things: "After all, if I am simply driven by my genes or by my glands, how can I be responsible for my sex life?" Such talk represents refusal to be a man or a woman. "After all, if I am simply a middle-class white American, how can I have any knowledge or awareness of responsibility about the economic crisis which is being revealed just below the level of our racial revolution?" Whenever I speak this way, I am simply confirming communist theory. I am saying that I am not a free man but a product of my economic and historical environment; I am bowing to fate. But the Bible insists that God has made us free from fate.

Here, perhaps, is the real scandal of the gospel, the thing that is really hard to understand and hard to believe: that in Jesus of Nazareth God has made us free from fate, from all the forces which distort and pervert human life. God's program in history is to "defatalize" human life, to put man's life into man's own hands and to give him the terrible responsibility of running it.

So God also makes us free for life, and not many of us are really ready to accept that kind of freedom. We are afraid of the freedom of defatalization. But to live with responsible freedom in today's world is what we mean by biblical faith. To answer God's call today is to respond in freedom and in responsibility to the tumultuous events of our times through which he is calling us. Faith does not mean attaching one's signature to a series of religious propositions, whether Catholic or Unitarian or Baptist; it means living one's life in the freedom and responsibility that God makes possible. Many of us don't want this. We would much rather be ruled by either our glands or our class status, for such a way of life is much easier than thinking.

God makes us free. This is what the Bible means when it talks about the defeat of principalities and powers. It is what the Apostles' Creed means when it says that Jesus "descended into hell." The gods have been banished. They are dead, and all that we have left is a man on a cross, a man who won't intervene when we try to kill him — hardly the way a normal god operates! But Jesus discloses a God who won't intervene even when we try to take our own collective lives, a God who turns man's story over to man. This God is defatalizing our whole history. He is making us free and responsible. He is pressing us into a situation in which we can no longer blame anyone else for what goes wrong, including him. This is freedom.

Possibly after this description of freedom we might well decide that we don't want it. Such is our privilege. God never violates our personalities; he permits us to stay in bondage if we want to do so.

3. The final constituent in the *shalom* which is God's Word for man is HOPE. Hopeful expectation characterizes *shalom*. It is hope which Martin Luther King describes in his dream. It is hope which the biblical prophet describes in his picture of the kingdom of *shalom*. The Spanish Christian philosopher, Miguel Unamuno, insists that if you want to know what a man's real faith is, you must find out not what he says he believes but what he really hopes for. The object of

our hope gives clearer indication of our relationship to biblical faith than what we do on Sunday morning, or what we say we believe. What do we hope for, for ourselves and for our fellowmen, for our country, for our world, for our generation? Is it for God's *shalom?* Is it for the kind of terrible and responsible freedom that comes from living in a defatalized world — the world in which God has handed the reins over to us and won't come down from the cross even to save himself? Do we hope for this, or for something less demanding?

Together with reconciliation and freedom, hope is one of the constituents of this rich word *shalom.* But, in seeing them together with what we said in Chapter 1, it is crucial to recall that God is working his reconciliation *in the world.* It is the world's renewal in which the church is privileged to participate. The church is not the only community of renewal, but it participates gladly and thankfully in the totality of that renewal which God makes possible in the world. Therefore our hope is also a hope for the world.

The Hebrews were liberated from the pharaoh not just to be free, but to be a servant people, to return once again to the world as free men so that they could be servants. They were called to bring hope to the whole world. Likewise God calls us out of a particular relationship to the world, a relationship of bondage, not just to get us out but to send us back into another relationship to the world. We live in the world as those who hope for and work for the renewal of the world.

It was the mistake of our pietistic forebears to believe that simply *coming out* of the world was enough —

"don't be worldly." They forgot the second half which was to *go back into* the world, to identify with it, to love it, to serve it. It was the mistake of our liberal forefathers to believe that coming out of the world was unnecessary — that man could serve the world without first being freed from it. But God's way involves a two-way motion — to free his people from captivity and, in turn, to make them servants. He frees the church *from* the gods of the world, *from* the powers that decimate and deteriorate life, so that his people can live *in* the world as its servants.

Similarly, our hope is not for the church nor for ourselves; it is for the world, that God will make the world new, that God will reconstruct and reconstitute the world in the shape of his *shalom.*

We need a theology of hope today. In discussions with Christians, Marxists frequently concede that their doctrine of man is insufficient and say they want to learn something of the biblical understanding of man. But then they ask Christians about the Christian hope. Is it only a hope for something beyond this life? Beyond history? If it is, then a modern man who is oriented toward *this* history and *this* life has no interest. Here the Marxist critique pulls us up short. If we really examine the story of God's *shalom* in the development of the Old Testament, and if we really listen to what Jesus says about his kingdom, then we can no longer pretend that God's *shalom* is something that comes only beyond death or beyond history. We must now begin to make clear what our hope is for this world. What *is* the hope that the church has for its whole environment — God's world? This is the most pressing question Christians must deal with today.

We began by describing God's *shalom,* and its constituent elements of reconciliation, peace, and hope. Let us now turn for a moment to the church and ask about its relation to God's Word for his world.

What is the church? Again read through the Bible and see the enormous variety of different symbols and figures used to describe the church. It is a body, a vine, a plant, a people. Let us consider for a moment the church as a people, the people of God, the *laos theon.* To do so, we must immediately discard any notion that the church is a building, or an organization, or a budget, or a denomination or council, or any of the other things which it is not. The church can *use* buildings, though more frequently I think it is used *by* them, for it got along very well for three centuries without buildings. The church can *use* budgets and programs and organizations, but it is more frequently used *by* them than it uses them. So we must begin by saying that the church is a people. It is people who live their lives in the world like everyone else, for the church is a part of the world, and thus also a sphere of God's activity. It is part of the theater of God's reconciling work; it is the locus of the Christian life and of all the things we have said about the world in the first chapter. But we can say all this about the church because it is that part of the world which is privileged to recognize and to celebrate what God is doing in and for the *whole* world.

This, then, is the church: a people who live their lives in a pattern of scattering and then coming together, only to scatter again and come together again, very much as the heart sends out oxygenated blood to nourish every little capillary, then receives it again to be recharged with oxygen from the lungs for recirculation. This is the true pattern of the church's life, gathering and scattering, and our mistake has been to identify it only with the gathered phase. We have talked very mistakenly about "going to church" on Sunday, "staying for church" after Sunday school, and "belonging to the church." But we *are* the church and we gather on Sunday in what our Baptist forefathers quite rightly called the "meeting house," the place where God's people gather but only to scatter again. But what is this people supposed to be doing in the world? What is God's intention for them?

To answer this question one has only to read the founding document of the church which is seen in 1 Peter 2:9: "But you are a chosen race, a royal priesthood, a holy nation, God's own people, that you may declare the wonderful deeds of him who called you out of darkness into his marvelous light." If we look in the King James Version, we will find that it reads like this: "That ye should show forth the praises of him who hath called you out of the darkness into his marvelous light." So, in one passage we have to "show forth" and in the other we have to "declare" the virtue of God.

It is strikingly appropriate that this word translated either "declare" or "show forth" should be so ambiguous. The church is not simply a talking people, a people who declare and proclaim things. It is not simply a *showing* people who demonstrate things. It is both a demonstrating *and* a declaring people, a people who are as good as their word, whose deeds speak, whose words act. This is the character of the word which the church has. The church's word is the echo of God's Word. God's Word comes first and the church has its *shalom* when it echoes that Word, not simply by talking about it but by demonstrating it.

One of the things every tourist in East Berlin sees is Karl Marx Allee, formerly called Stalinallee. It was built by the Communist regime in East Germany for a specific purpose, to *demonstrate* to visitors what the Communist society will be like when it is completed. It is the "street of the future." When Communism has fully arrived, they say, all the world will look like Karl Marx Allee. Something of this idea is present in the church. The church should be the society of the future, a demonstration of what is to come.

Also, just as Karl Marx Allee is supposed to blend invisibly into the future society, so also the church is not the last word that God has for man. It is a provisional thing, a word on the way to something else. Appropriately, therefore, we began this little book with the world and not with the church; and we will not finish with the church, because the church is not the *fulfillment* of God's plan, but a *stage* on the way. It is a discardable, provisional stage, and that fact puts us in our place. Just as Karl Marx Allee is a description of the new order as the Communists understand it, the church is a description or demonstration of the new order as the Christian understands it. The church should be that group in which anyone can see a corporate life demonstrating the *shalom* of God. It should be a sign of the kingdom, an indication of the things that are to come, a demonstration community, to show to the entire world what God is doing for it.

It is also the privilege of the church to *celebrate* what God is doing not only for it but for the whole world. This is the first assignment of God's people, as we can clearly see when we read the Psalms and when we recall what the early Christians did. They were celebrating something that God was doing, and they often celebrated it in a very raucous way. It is still the job of the church to *tell* the world what God is doing for it; there is also a place for the articulated word. For instance, one can show his girl friend in any number of ways that he loves her (even in lavish ways), but somehow or other it is only when this message is expressed through spoken words that something happens to the couple. A word does something to cement the relationship which all the symbols and acts and demonstrations somehow don't do. So it is the church's frightening responsibility to say the word to the world — the word *shalom*, the Word of Jesus of Nazareth.

We can't live without words. The question is: Where is this word found? It is found only when Christians live in solidarity with the world. Christians are those who can't be explained in the world's terms, because they are not living simply for their class or race, their national or sexual interests. They present an enigma to the world, an inexplicable thing which people finally have to ask them about. Then comes the time for speaking. Among the Hebrews only once a year, at the high festival within the holy of holies, the priest was allowed to utter the name of God. We could well recover some of this verbal restraint, for sometimes talking about God is mere prattle. On the other hand, however, we should be ready to answer when the world asks the reason for the faith that is in us. It may be that the opportunity given us by God to speak his Word comes when we are found in the struggle for social justice now going on in our world. Someone asks: What are you doing anyway on this picket line? What are you getting out of it? Why is it your fight? What are you doing here in Asia or Africa helping Asians or Africans to some kind of dignity, some kind of freedom? Why is it your interest? This may be our God-given opportunity to say the word however reticently and stumblingly. The blunt question, "What the hell are you doing here?" may be the way in which twentieth-century man asks, "What must I do to be saved?"

What are we doing in the world where God's *shalom* is now breaking in, where God's new kingdom, his new regime is taking shape? What are we doing here where the signs of the kingdom are appearing? Often the reason why we are not asked this question is simply that we are not there. We have failed to fall in behind God and his rather quick pace in our time, and God is calling us now to hurry up and get in step with him.

chapter 4

SACRAMENT: SUFFERING WITH GOD IN HIS WORLD

As soon as we use the word "sacrament" today, we transport ourselves into a self-consciously religious discussion. We have left the real world, and we are now in a little world of our own. The word "sacrament" comes to us dragging all kinds of pious connotations. It is definitely a "holy word," which makes us think immediately of communion, prayer, worship, and the so-called "devotional life." Because this whole complex of practices seems so remote from life, the program we have designated as "despiritualization" or "de-etherealization" becomes exceedingly difficult. However, we are not alone in our difficulties. Elisabeth Adler, a former staff member of the World Student Christian Federation, writing in the *Student World* says:

> Of all the different aspects of the life of the church, worship seems to be that furthest removed from everyday, secular life,

and that most threatened by the growing secularization of our culture. . . . There are few of us who do not at times feel something of the estrangement of the secular world from the Church's worship.[1]

We can only agree with Miss Adler, and our agreement makes it very difficult to deal with the subject, except in a highly provisional way. But let us make a start.

We have referred already to Martin Luther King's *Letter from the Birmingham Jail.* Another letter from another jail may help us begin to grapple with the problem of what to do with "worship" in a secular age. This letter was written from Berlin's grim Tegel prison by Dietrich Bonhoeffer, the German pastor-martyr who was murdered by the Nazis. Here is an excerpt:

Another month gone! Do you find that time flies as I do here? It often amazes me. . . . The thing that keeps coming back to me as I sit here is, what *is* Christianity, and, indeed, what *is* Christ for us today? The time when men could be told everything by means of words, whether theological or simply pious, is over and so is the time of inwardness and conscience, which is to say the time of religion as such. We are proceeding towards a time of no religion at all: men as they are now simply cannot be religious any more. Even those who honestly describe themselves as "religious" do not in the least act up to it. . . . What we call Christianity has always been a pattern — perhaps a true pattern — of religion. But if one day it becomes apparent that this *a priori* "premise" simply does not exist but was an historical and temporary form of human self-expression, i.e., if we reach the stage of being radically without religion — and I think this is more or less the case already . . . what does that mean for Christianity? . . . How can Christ become the Lord even of those with no religion?[2]

[1] No. 1, 1963, p. 89.
[2] Dietrich Bonhoeffer, *Prisoner for God,* edited by Eberhard Bethge and translated by Reginald H. Fuller (New York: The Macmillan Company, 1953), pp. 121-123.

Religion is no more than the garment of Christianity, and even that garment has had a variety of different aspects in different periods. What then is a religion-less Christianity? How do we speak of God without religion? What is the significance of the secularization of the world for the church or for preaching? What is the significance of worship in a religionless world? These questions an ever increasing number of us are asking. In attempting to find honest answers, we have to start much further back than most of us ordinarily would do.

Let us begin simply by taking the word "worship" and seeing what it has come to mean today. Then let us look at the Old and New Testaments to see whether today's meaning bears any resemblance to what was happening then in the life of the people of God. The word "worship" comes from the Saxon *weorthscipe,* which means "homage" or "obedience," or, as *The Interpreter's Dictionary of the Bible* puts it, "the attitude and activity designed to recognize and describe the worth of the person or thing to which homage is addressed." [8] The same reference goes on to say: "Here 'worship' is used to describe the activities and attitudes, the behavior, proper to the sanctuary; in Christian parlance 'divine worship.' "

This definition dramatizes our problem. Did it ever occur to the writer of this definition that it was precisely to abolish this "sanctuary mentality" that Jesus lived his whole career? that the message of the New Testa-

[8] *The Interpreter's Dictionary of the Bible* (New York and Nashville: Abingdon Press, 1962), vol. 4, p. 879.

ment is that there isn't any sanctuary any more? that there isn't any place set aside and sanctified in a religious sense apart from everyday life? Jesus repeatedly violated sanctuaries. He went into the temple turning over tables; he approvingly cited the story of David eating the holy bread (shewbread). To him there was no such thing as a special time, place, and procedure for signifying obedience and homage to God.

The story is that as Jesus was hanging on the cross the veil of the temple was rent, thus demolishing the division between the Holy of Holies (the sanctuary) and the outer court (representing the world). Paul made this point very clearly in the text that we referred to earlier, when he said that in Christ the wall has been broken down. Christ has been crucified on the cross, and with him the law — the law representing the religious sector of life. Thus it is the world which is the locale for Christian worship. Worship characterizes the entire life of the people of God, including the attitudes and activities involved in their work. In the Old Testament relatively little importance is attached to worship in the narrow sense; that is the gathering at appointed times and places for ritual activity.

Walter J. Harrelson in his article in Hastings' revised *Dictionary of the Bible* under the word "worship" says that the worship or service of God required no special place, time, or priesthood, since God was conceived to be "almost a member of the tribe, one who accompanied the people in their wanderings." [4] Harrelson is

[4] James Hastings, ed., *Dictionary of the Bible*, revised edition by Frederick Grant and H. H. Rowley (New York: Charles Scribner's Sons, 1963), p. 1043.

certainly right. The Canaanite deities required cultic worship, ritual activity; but Yahweh, the God of the Jews, required something far more demanding.

In understanding this difference today, we have enormous difficulties. The reason is that the Old Testament we have is in the English language and there aren't very many people who can read Hebrew. If they could, they would find that there are six *different* Hebrew words which are translated with the same English word "worship." (This is the same difficulty we found with the word "world" in the New Testament.) The result has been to project into the English translation of the Old Testament a false, over-spiritualized, and cultic understanding of man's relationship to God. Let us look for a moment at some of the Hebrew words which are all translated "worship" in English, and notice just how different they are.

The first word is the Hebrew *hishtahweh,* which meant "to prostrate oneself," for example before a king. It was the act of symbolic deference suggesting obedience to the sovereign. The closest parallel in our time would be the military salute, or our pledge of allegiance to the flag, the kind of symbolic act whereby one's loyalty is expressed. This was not necessarily a religious act at all.

The second term which frequently is translated "worship" is simply the word *abhadh* "to serve." It is related to the regular word for servant, manservant, or maidservant; or it can designate service in a military unit. To the Hebrews it meant the activity of living in service, in obedience to someone. Thus the translation of this word as "worship" proves extremely misleading today. Even when it is translated as "serve," a great deal of confusion results. "Serve the Lord with gladness! Come into his presence with singing," we read before a cultic worship service. But this is the wrong time to read it; instead, it should be read before we go *out from* the worship service. "Serve the Lord with gladness," does not mean a cultic activity, but service in the literal sense.

There are words in the Old Testament that do refer to cultic acts (what we usually mean when we say "worship"), but they are very frequently used in a negative sense, to describe what people do to the idols and not what they do to the living God. Take for example Ezekiel 20:31-32:

> When you offer your gifts and sacrifice your sons by fire, you defile yourselves with all your idols to this day. And shall I be inquired of by you, O house of Israel? As I live, says the Lord God, I will not be inquired of by you. "What is in your mind shall never happen — the thought, 'Let us be like the nations, like the tribes of the countries, and worship wood and stone.'..."

The word translated "worship" here in the phrase "worship wood and stone" appears only three or four times in the whole Bible, always in a negative way. This cultic worship is what the idols and the gods of the Canaanites sought, whereas the living God sought those who would *serve* him and by their service would indicate that he was their sovereign.

This is not to say the Hebrews had no cultic worship. They did, but it was not as central to them as we have often made out. Take for example the Sabbath, which we associate with churchgoing. We think that for the Jews it was also a kind of a cultic or ritual activity. Didn't they go on every seventh day to some temple or synagogue or something? This is the picture we ordinarily have, but the answer is simply, "No." Once again let us turn to Walter Harrelson, one of our best Old Testament scholars, as he corrects this view: "The remarkable fact is that nowhere in the Old Testament is a prescribed ritual for Sabbath observance to be found." [8] The Sabbath is depicted as a day of rest and rejoicing in the goodness and faithfulness of Yahweh, of God, not as a day for ritual activity. It was a day for celebrating the goodness of God and staying home with the wife and kids. But, when people want to spend Sunday in this way today, we often tell them that they are not observing the Sabbath rightly!

We can probably sum up the whole spirit of Old Testament worship by quoting Isaiah 58:4-8:

> Behold, you fast only to quarrel and to fight
> and to hit with wicked fist.
> Fasting like yours this day
> will not make your voice to be heard on high.
> Is such the fast that I choose,
> a day for a man to humble himself?
> Is it to bow down his head like a rush,
> and to spread sackcloth and ashes under him?
> Will you call this a fast,
> and a day acceptable to the Lord?
> "Is not this the fast that I choose:
> to loose the bonds of wickedness,
> to undo the throngs of the yoke,
> to let the oppressed go free,
> and to break every yoke?

[8] *Ibid.*, p. 1044.

> Is it not to share your bread with the hungry,
>   and bring the homeless poor into your house;
> when you see the naked, to cover him,
>   and not to hide yourself from your own flesh?
> Then shall your light break forth like the dawn,
>   and your healing shall spring up speedily;
> your righteousness shall go before you,
>   the glory of the Lord shall be your rear guard.

Now let us go to the New Testament and see what "worship" means there. The fact is that the earliest gatherings of the followers of Jesus were *not* worship services in our sense at all. The early church people gathered for what they called the "breaking of bread," that is, the sharing of a meal with each other. They had bread, and wine too if they could afford it. They talked and exchanged ideas with each other. They recalled the words of Jesus. They probably read messages from other groups of Christians and from the Apostles. They certainly gave thanks for the bread according to the ancient Jewish tradition, but their gathering was hardly a cultic thing. When Paul writes to the young church at Corinth in 1 Corinthians 11:18-22, he says:

> For, in the first place, when you assemble as a church, I hear that there are divisions among you; and I partly believe it, for there must be factions among you in order that those who are genuine among you may be recognized. When you meet together, it is not the Lord's supper that you eat. For in eating, each one goes ahead with his own meal, and one is hungry and another is drunk. What! Do you not have houses to eat and drink in? Or do you despise the church of God and humiliate those who have nothing? What shall I say to you? Shall I commend you in this? No, I will not.

It is clear that Paul was not warning these people against eating and drinking, nor even against having a full meal when they came together as Christians. Rather he was telling the ones who got there first not to eat it all and drink it all, but to leave a fair share for those who were late. He wanted everyone's hunger and thirst to be satisfied. But what has happened now to what we call our "communion service"? It has become progressively smaller until no one could possibly have his hunger satisfied. Certainly the earliest followers of Jesus would have been very much puzzled to hear that their supper was a cultic "worship service." For them the whole necessity of religious acts of worship — for a cultus — had been abolished by Jesus. Cultic worship means engaging in activities designed to influence and gain mercy from God. But God had *already* shown mercy. Cultic worship means gathering at certain prescribed times at particular holy places to follow an accepted ritual procedure. But all of that was gone. It was precisely that from which they had been liberated in Jesus of Nazareth. He was the high priest who had made the final sacrifice, and there was no need to make any more.

It is also clear from our best sources that the spirit in these meetings was rather uproarious. Remember that in the second chapter of Acts some of the bystanders are quoted as saying of the people assembled on Pentecost, "They are filled with new wine." This is a good description of the kind of spirit which must have been present. Such sessions probably resembled the victory celebrations of a football team more than most of the worship services that we have attended. We have developed impossibly rigid ideas about what is a worship service and what isn't. For example, there is hardly a person who has not gone through this experience: At a student conference someone says, "Now this evening we are going to have a worship service, but we are going to start with some good fun songs. Then there will be a gradual transition into a mood of worship." What is this phony "mood of worship"? All of the celebration, the victory, the uproariousness is left behind as someone dims the light and we are now in the mood of worship.

It should perhaps be just the opposite. We should start with this kind of solemnity and sadness and then modulate into something more like a joyful kind of folk singing. I recall once when I was at Green Lake, Wisconsin, for a conference, and we had a folk sing in the lobby. Christians were gathering together singing for joy. We sang "We Shall Overcome," a song that expresses the hope which is part of God's *shalom*. Then we sang about God's drowning the Egyptians, "Pharoah's Army Got Drowned," and "He's Got the Whole World in His Hands." These songs were very good theology. Then someone said, "Oh-oh! Time for the worship service." We all filed out over to the vesper circle, the organ came in with its tremolo, and we sang some songs about our own souls. That was supposed to be "worship." But it wasn't!

Of course we must concede that even among the earliest Christians something began to develop which soon produced a special priestly class, and a set of activities which were to happen recurrently at specific times and places. Baptism and the breaking of bread took on more and more of a cultic shape. Some of the characteristics of the Greek mystery religions were brought in. But why should we assume that this growth was natural or even healthy? We can feel perfectly free to be liberated from our rigid, ecclesiasticized notion of worship simply by seeing what these early Christians did. There was a wide variety. There were differences between the Jewish Christians and the non-Jewish Christians, between the church at Jerusalem and the church in Galatia. Paul makes it clear that there was no uniformity when he talks about "your reasonable service" (Romans 12:1, as in KJV; the word "service" becomes "worship" in RSV and NEB). What is "reasonable worship"? Prayer? Hymns? No, it is "to present your bodies as a living sacrifice." He then goes on to list what we would call a social action or a Christian responsibility program: "Practice hospitality." "Rejoice with those who rejoice, weep with those who weep." "Repay no one evil for evil." This is what Paul calls "your reasonable worship."

Paul is not creating a new idea of worship here; he is simply being faithful to his own Hebrew tradition, as it has been expressed by the prophets over the centuries. But in other passages Paul does do something different. He describes what we would call "worship services" in *secular* terminology, and what we would call "service in the world" in *religious* or sacral terminology, using words that we ordinarily apply to worship. One of the reports of the 1963 World Council of Churches' Faith and Order meeting in Montreal states that Paul introduced quite secular terms for describing the worship act and worship gatherings of the church, while he used cultic and sacrificial terms for describing the everyday life of those who were living in the world.

The impact of the gospel on the traditional distinction between sacred and secular was to turn the whole thing upside down and inside out. The whole contrast between the holy and the everyday, between the religious and the worldly, was simply reversed. What had been thought of as religious and cultic was now described as secular. What had been derogated as belonging to the common realm was now viewed and described in terms of worship, praise, thanksgiving, and the offering of sacrifices. Thus the gospel of Jesus did not introduce a new religion; rather it utterly demolished the very basis on which all religions, all religious views of life function; that is, the distinction between the sacred and the profane.

Now some people, such as Bonhoeffer, say we are coming to the end of the religious period of human history. The impact of this biblical demolition of the distinction between the sacred and secular has been so far-reaching that it has now touched all of our lives, and the characteristically religious element is disappearing. So, Bonhoeffer asks, how can we have a religionless gospel? How can Jesus be the Lord of man without religion?

This is precisely the issue we must face. We used to say, during the religious days, that all of life had become sacramental. It may be more accurate in the period which we are entering to say that now all of life has been turned over to man. All of it has been made human, made secular. The world has been allowed to become the world. If Bonhoeffer is right in his contention (and there are indications that he is), it is quite obvious that we are in a time of transition. During this time of transition we cannot insist that people be either religious or postreligious if they are to understand and follow Jesus Christ. The wall which has separated the people — the religious from the nonreligious — is one of the walls which Jesus breaks down by his *shalom*. But it is one of the most difficult walls of all for us to break. There are many people for whom the cultic worship service which we have inherited from our fathers has an enormous significance, and there are others for whom, struggle as they will, such services have no meaning at all. We are summoned by the *shalom* which Jesus brings, not to think that either of these kinds of people is within or without — not to think that the nonreligious man is more sophisticated or more mature than the religious man or vice versa. This barrier is just as high, perhaps, as the barrier of race, of nation, or of class. It is a wall which, as reconciling agents, we have to break down.

Now, let us say a couple of things about what we have been traditionally taught about so-called sacraments — that is, about baptism and the Lord's Supper. Let us begin with baptism. There are three images by which the New Testament presents interpretations of baptism.

1. The first of these images is that of the escape from Egyptian bondage. It is found in 1 Corinthians 10:1-4:

> I want you to know, brethren, that our fathers were all under the cloud, and all passed through the sea, and all were baptized into Moses in the cloud and in the sea, and all ate the same supernatural food and all drank the same supernatural drink. For they drank from the supernatural Rock which followed them, and the Rock was Christ.

Paul sees baptism in the image of the passage of the people of Israel through the Red Sea, out of captivity and into freedom. We have already said that the passage of the people of Israel out of captivity was to enable them to become servants. Therefore, baptism is first of all a symbol of our being freed from our bondage to the world, dying to our minor loyalties, dying to our little gods, dying to the infirm values that we have made supreme — in order to be freed for service to the world. Baptism is becoming free to be involved in the world without any cares about our own identity, our own labels, our own morals, our own religious status: free for the world and free for our fellowman. This is what the exodus was and this is what baptism signifies.

2. The second image of baptism in the New Testament is the baptism of Jesus himself. What was the baptism of Jesus? It was *not* Jesus' decision to join the religious community of his day, as it has become for us. Markus Barth, after a good deal of study on the baptism of Jesus, suggests that for Jesus the act of being baptized in the dirty river Jordan at the hands of this unkempt prophet from the wilderness, John the Baptist, was a *rejection* of the mediated religion of the temple. He turned his back on the temple, went out of the city and down to the Jordan, and identified

himself with this mob of anticlerical rabble who were the followers of John. This is very stiff medicine to take — that to follow Jesus into the waters of baptism means to turn one's back on the mediated religion of the day and to identify one's self with the rabble, with the alcoholics, with those without the law — and yet the best understanding of the meaning of Jesus' baptism is exactly this. He identifies himself, says Markus Barth, with those who "had nothing to confess but their sins."

But what have we done to baptism? We have turned it completely around. We have made it a rejection of those who have nothing to confess but their sins; it has become an entry into a religious community, an antiworldly community, the very opposite of what baptism meant for Jesus himself. To follow Jesus in the waters of baptism, is to follow him into solidarity with the world, into solidarity with those "without the law."

3. The third symbol or image used in the New Testament for baptism is the crucifixion of Jesus. Paul uses this in various writings, including Romans 6:3-4: "Do you not know that all of us who have been baptized into Christ Jesus were baptized into his death? We were buried therefore with him by baptism into death, so that as Christ was raised from the dead by the glory of the Father, we too might walk in newness of life." The crucifixion of Jesus was a radical breaking-through of all the religious and conventional taboos, the most desegregated event imaginable. Jesus' death summarizes his whole life. It was a constant effort to make these labels and barriers — Pharisees, non-Pharisees, publicans, Jews, Greeks, Gentiles — all of these totally

irrelevant. It was to remind men that they were brothers, that they now were citizens of the new kingdom in which these minor loyalties to other kingdoms, to other realms, were relativized and abolished. Walking in newness of life means now to see the world "crucifixionally," to see the world as the place in which the crucifixion of Jesus goes on today, tomorrow, and day after day. To identify ourselves with the death of Jesus is to move out and to participate in this continuing crucifixion. To walk in newness of life is to share in death.

But some people ask, "Isn't baptism pretty archaic anyway? Something we can dispose of?" It might be, but it might *not* be. We live in the era of the demonstration, of saying things to people by visual dramatic enactment, and baptism is a way of saying that we identify ourselves with this kind of death and with the continuing effects and workings of this crucifixion in the world today. It demonstrates to the world our solidarity with the world.

The next question to ask is whether our *form* of baptism is correct. I don't mean how much water do we use, or any of that. I mean, is it going to be necessary for us now to find a new way of dramatically portraying to the worldly ones our solidarity with them and with the Jesus of Nazareth whose crucifixion continues as he lives with them? Christians didn't think up baptism. They simply took it over from their environment, giving it a new twist. Is it possible that God may be suggesting to us today that we find a *new* way of saying the same thing, a new way of dramatically showing our solidarity with the suffering and the exploited of the world, a new way of declaring our participation in the ongoing crucifixion? How can our baptism today, which is so cultic and so spiritualized, be once again planted just as deeply in the world as the original cross was planted on that hillside outside Jerusalem? That is a question for which I have no answer.

Now what about the Lord's Supper? Again it is clear to me that, when Jesus refers to his "cup" ("This cup is the new covenant in my blood"), he is *not* talking about the cup in his hand, but about his crucifixion. Remember that, just after the story of the Last Supper, Jesus is depicted praying in Gethsemane: "My father, if it be possible, let this cup pass from me; nevertheless, not as I will, but as thou wilt" (Matthew 26:39). To drink of this cup is to share in what Bonhoeffer calls "the suffering of God in the world." If we are laboring under the delusion that he refers simply to a cup of wine or fruit juice and that by sharing this we share in the newness of life and in the resurrection and in the crucifixion, this is a very dangerous self-deception. Whenever Jesus refers to a cup, throughout the New Testament, he always means his death, his crucifixion, and this is the cup in which we are invited to share.

We still have much to learn by a study of the sacraments (or what some Christians call "ordinances"):

1. First, notice that the sacraments are not manna coming down from heaven untouched by human hands. Notice that they are not apples that you pick off a tree, nor water that you draw from a spigot. These are things which must be planted, grown, and manufac-

tured: Wine must be squeezed, and bread must be baked. They have to be packaged and then transported by truck drivers over highways on which people work, which policemen patrol, and brought eventually to us. In other words, for the elements through which Jesus is present for us, we are *totally dependent on the world!* We can't do without the world. We can't do without the truck driver, the policeman, the baker, the wrapper, or any of the people who make this substance available for us. Jesus is present for us today in their world, as we can easily learn from a casual observation of the elements.

Where did Jesus get that bread and wine that was used on the night of the first Lord's Supper? Someone must have gone out to a local bakery, to the wine shop in Jerusalem, and come home with a bottle of wine and a loaf of bread. Maybe they sent downstairs for a waiter and he brought it up. But they didn't manufacture it themselves. They were dependent, as we are today, on the world to provide us with the elements within which we meet our Lord.

2. Second, these elements are broken and poured out. It is in the *breaking* of these things and in the *pouring out* that we see the dramatized way in which Jesus is present for us in the world. None of the arguments about transubstantiation and consubstantiation make any sense at all to us, because in our world we don't think in these categories of substance any more. We must focus on the *action.* When Jesus took the bread, he *broke* it and said, "This is my body *broken* for you." It is in the brokenness, the sharing of abuse, of ridi-

cule, of being despised and rejected of men, that we partake in this bread. The same principle holds true for the cup as it is poured out. Our powerlessness, our vulnerability in allowing ourselves to be broken and poured out is what we can learn here from these elements.

3. Third, the elements must be eaten, taken into our systems. Digested, they become a part of our corpuscles and molecules. We do not "observe" the wine and the bread; we make them a part of our life.

4. Fourth, these elements are not spiritual items, but solid, substantial things that you can get a grip on, that you can see and eat: "O taste and see that the Lord is good!" Our physical presence at the point of hostility, of alienation, of brokenness, as the ones who try to stand there with healing and wholeness witnessing to God's *shalom* and God's reconciliation, is what is needed. The community of Taizé in France sends out its members to live wherever there are points of political tension and exploitation. They are there with their *physical* presence, not with "a spiritual presence," nor with "a religious interest." It is the physical body which stands there. This approach is very important when we think about the demonstrations and picket lines of our day. All the spiritual friendliness and all the religious sympathy doesn't add up to one physical body standing on a picket line. What we can learn from the elements of the Lord's Supper is that something physical is present. The suffering of God in the world that Bonhoeffer talks about, and into which we are called to participate, is just as physical as that.

There have always been people who have worshiped and people who have not worshiped. There have always been people interested in and sustained by cultic activity, and people who aren't (I think there are more and more of the latter kind today). Biblical faith is not distinguished by the fact that its people worship, but by reconciliation, by freedom, by hope, by its demonstration of God's *shalom*. It is not a particular religion among others; it is something that can cross even the line between human beings who have found themselves in separate camps. It unites cultic and noncultic personalities in Jesus, our *shalom*. It radically relativizes the importance of a cultic community. Circumcision or noncircumcision, says Paul, is not the issue. By their fruits you shall know them, says Jesus.

The church is a people who gather together and then scatter. It will always be this kind of people, but the character of what happens in the gathering and in the going forth may vary from age to age. Christians come together to sing, to be sustained by their mutual presence, to acknowledge the sovereign to whom they are obedient. But Christians must remain very open about the character of what happens when they do gather.

The church of the future will be smaller, more mobile, more flexible, much more disciplined, much more various in the ways in which it celebrates. It will be much more joyful, less solemn than we are when we come together. It will be much less preacher-oriented, much less cultic, much more open to discussion and give-and-take. This is the church we are moving toward and it may be the kind that will answer Bonhoeffer's question.

Let me close this chapter with another excerpt from his letters from prison:

Man is challenged to participate in the sufferings of God at the hands of a godless world.

He must plunge himself into the life of a godless world, without attempting to gloss over its ungodliness with a veneer of religion or trying to transfigure it. . . . To be a Christian does not mean to be religious in a particular way, to cultivate some particular form of ascetism . . . but to be a man. It is not some religious act which makes a Christian what he is, but participation in the suffering of God in the life of the world. . . .

Jesus does not call men to a new religion, but to life. What is the nature of that life, that participation in the powerlessness of God in the world? More about that next time, I hope.[*]

But there wasn't any next time for Bonhoeffer. Shortly after he wrote these lines, the Gestapo entered his cell and he was executed. There was never any next time, because instead of simply *talking* about participation in the suffering of God in the world, he participated.

[*] Bonhoeffer, *op.cit.*, pp. 166-167.

chapter 5

MINISTRY: WORKING WITH GOD IN HIS WORLD

So far we have dealt with four salient issues: (1) the world-in-revolution as the arena of God's action, (2) man's slothful refusal to live up to his full manhood, (3) the Word as God's gift to his world, and (4) sacrament as suffering with God in his world. We now come to the ministry of the church, the shape of God's people in the world. In every instance, our discussion has been sharply characterized by what theologians call a "Christological" emphasis. We have suggested that in Jesus of Nazareth we encounter a God who discloses himself through activities that threaten the status quo, through something like what we now call revolution. We have insisted that God's Word for the world *is* Jesus of Nazareth, a lived Word, a man whose life we have described with the old Jewish word *shalom*. As constituent parts of the word *shalom* we have listed reconciliation, freedom, and hope. Finally, we have described Jesus himself as the only real sacrament. He is the one through whose sacrificial action God touches and renews his world. Our partaking of the sacrament, which is usually understood very religiously, really means our participation in the suffering of God in today's world.

All of this is very important as we try to describe what the mission or ministry of the church must be today. It is important because the ministry of the church is no more and no less than participation in the mission of God. This concept means that the first thing the church must always do is to find out where God is on the move in his world today, and then make all possible haste to be there with him. It does not mean, however, that the church must look back and forth between the world and somewhere else. The meaning of the life of Jesus of Nazareth is that God and the world can no longer be separated. We do not have to look back and forth now in harried anxiety between the world and God, trying to apply the one to the other. As Bonhoeffer once said:

> Whoever set eyes on the body of Jesus Christ in faith can never again speak of the world as though it were lost, as though it were separated from Christ. . . . It is only in Christ that the world is what it is. . . . It is only in the midst of the world that Christ is Christ.[1]

We have been emphasizing all along that in a secular age the mission of the church must assume a secular style. This idea should come as no surprise. God's becoming man in Jesus represents a kind of radical secu-

[1] Dietrich Bonhoeffer, *Ethics*, edited by Eberhard Bethge (New York: The Macmillan Company, 1955), p. 71.

larization. God laid aside his religiousness, his divine attributes, and took upon himself the form of a servant. This was a secular form. The church must learn to do the same today. But how is it possible to have a "non-religious" ministry? Isn't that a contradiction in terms?

The answer to this question depends of course on what we mean by religion. There are four components of "religion" which come to mind, all of which stand in the way of an effective ministry today: (1) cultic worship, the gathering at stated times and places for ritually prescribed activity; (2) otherworldiness, the effort to escape the world in which God has placed us; (3) a division between the sacred and the secular; and (4) an inclusive worldview. All of these things are included in standard definitions of "religion," and all of them have been abolished and broken down by Jesus of Nazareth. Let us see how.

First, cultic worship is no longer necessary. The kind of thing the early Christians did when they got together was very much like what we do at a meal with friends and co-workers. This is not the ritual propitiation of a deity. It is the celebration of what God is doing in our world and of our privilege of being there with him. Second, there is no otherworldliness in Jesus. He announces a new worldliness, a new age, a new kingdom in which we are allowed to be citizens. He is its first representative. Third, the barrier between the sacred and the secular is not only abolished, but in many instances completely reversed. We now discuss our service in the world, our life during the week, in terms which before Jesus and Paul had been reserved for cultic and worship activities — sacrifice, pouring out, and so on. Fourth, as far as inclusive worldviews are concerned, the gospel calls them all into question and makes us live in total openness, without the crutches of systems and codes to fall back on.

The church is a people who have been entrusted with a Word. We said that God's Word to us is a living deed, a life lived, hands and feet walking among us, reconciliation making itself felt. Our word is a response to his Word. It is a demonstration, a participation and a celebration of God's *shalom*. But when does the church utter its word? In sermons? Rarely. Most often it is uttered today in response to the world's question, "What are you doing here?"

I was asked this question, "What are you doing here?" countless times during the year I worked as a link between the two cities of Berlin. I was asked because there were many people who thought that I was a bit mad traveling back and forth between West and East Berlin and taking the risk which is involved in this kind of activity. Many people thought I was stupid and foolish to be doing this thing if I didn't *have* to, if I didn't have relatives in the East Zone or some other reason that made it necessary for me to be there. I don't know how many times, sitting at the little interrogation office just inside the wall at Checkpoint Charlie, I was asked by other people waiting to be interrogated, and sometimes even asked by East German soldiers: "What are you doing here?" "Why are you doing this?" Of course, being interrogated by the Communists provided me an opportunity to speak, but my words would have fallen flat if they had been "religious" ones. My answer could not be to ask the Communist border guard to pray, at least not in traditional terms. It could not be an answer that would point him to a life beyond; he wanted a reply that would make sense to him, whether he believed it or not, in this world. It could not be an answer that allowed for a separation of his work (secular) from my work (sacred). Nor could it involve us in a debate between the Communist ideology and the so-called "Christian worldview."

No, my answer in this instance had always to vary with the person who asked me and the atmosphere of the situation in which it was asked. It had to be an answer that laid aside all claims on my part to superiority or judgment. It had to articulate our common involvement in the world in which God was working through a Communist border guard just as much as through me, although the guard was certainly unaware of this fact. My first job was to get across to him that the labels we use to separate ourselves from each other — "Communist," "Capitalist," "religious," "nonreligious" — have all been radically relativized by Jesus and his kingdom of *shalom*.

This refusal to allow a label to separate them from other people was what most vividly characterized the early Christians. In fact, they did not call *themselves* "Christians." That was a title tacked onto them by other people. We might well ask ourselves whether today the title "Christian" unduly separates us from other people. Perhaps like the earliest followers of Jesus we should not presume to call *ourselves* Christians, but should wait for other people, if they see some of the likeness of Christ in our lives, to make that kind of designation. We need to rediscover the sweeping refusal of labels which Jesus accomplished. His people were no longer Jews nor Greeks, no longer barbarians nor Scythians, no longer circumcised nor uncircumcised. All were one in a new kind of fraternal community which set aside these inherited labels. The difficulty is that the word "Christian" has developed in our time into a label which often separates us from other people. We must not be obsessed by labels, not even this one. It is true to the New Testament to say this: Wherever *any* label becomes an artificial barrier between myself and anyone else, it is better for me to sacrifice the label than to sacrifice a relationship.

This does not mean sacrificing our relationship to Jesus, nor our special bond with his people. It means remembering that *all* people are *in fact* his people, if they would only recognize and respond. It means developing a disciplined restraint in our speaking about the gospel. Here we can learn a great deal from a Roman Catholic order called "The Little Brothers and Sisters of Jesus." They are committed to work in the poorest sections of the industrial cities of France and among the Algerians in North Africa. One of the promises they make when they join their order is that they will never mention the name of Jesus unless someone asks them why they have chosen to live among the poor, the rejected, and the exploited. Perhaps this is the kind of reticence we should be learning today.

To go back for a moment to my conversations with

the Communist border guards: I had to learn to remember when I was speaking that I did not know whether this guard was in the church or not. Only God knows who is among the wheat and who is among the tares; such judgment is not a job which is handed over to us. In Jesus' story, the wheat and the tares are growing together in the field when the farmhands come to the farmer and say, "Shouldn't we go out and cut down the tares?" He replies: "No, don't do that, for at the same time you might also cut down the wheat. Let them both grow together until the harvest." Jesus thus warns us that it is none of our business to decide who is in and who is out. If a label becomes our means of judging who is in or out, then it is leading us to act in a way which is not appropriate for any human being.

In our particular time in history we need to devote more attention to those texts in the Bible which tell us about unclear boundaries between the church and the world, about the lack of assurance that we are "in" and someone else is "out." For example the text in Matthew 7:15 is one that should mean a lot to us today: "Beware of false prophets," Jesus says, "who come to you in sheep's clothing but inwardly are ravenous wolves." We might justifiably turn this around to read: "Beware of people who come to you in the costume of ravenous wolves but inwardly they may be prophets." There is also the text, "Not everyone who says to me 'Lord, Lord,' shall enter the kingdom of heaven, but he who does the will of my Father who is in heaven. On that day many will say to me, 'Lord, Lord, did we not prophesy in your name, and cast out demons in your name, and do many mighty works in your name?' And then will I declare to them, 'I never knew you; depart from me, you evildoers'" (Matthew 7:21-23). Then there were those very surprised people who at the Last Judgment would say to him, "Lord, when did we see thee hungry and feed thee, or thirsty and give thee drink? And when did we see thee a stranger and welcome thee, or naked and clothe thee? And when did we see thee sick or in prison and visit thee?" (Matthew 25:37-39). And he replied, "As you did it to one of the least of these, my brethren, you did it to me."

We can't take people entirely at their word, either when they say they are confessing Christ or when they say they are rejecting him. We just never know. The capstone of this whole group of very significant texts in the New Testament is the story that Jesus tells of the father who asks both of his sons to go and work in the field. One says, "I go," and doesn't go, whereas the other says "I go not," but in fact goes and works (Matthew 21:28-29). I don't believe we could find anywhere a more adequate picture of precisely what's going on in our world today. We do not need to concern ourselves unduly with scratching around to find something which differentiates us from someone else — a non-Christian, a nonreligious person, a nonbeliever. This is God's concern and not ours. Our business is to live in solidarity with these people, even though they may confuse us with someone else. Maybe they will mistake us for just do-gooders or humanists or something else, but remember that we will not be the first to have been so mistaken. Throughout Jesus' entire career, nobody, not even any of his closest followers, was quite clear as to his identity. Some of them thought he was a Zealot, some that he was an Essene, and Jesus himself was more interested in living in service and love and solidarity with his neighbors than making sure they knew his credentials. There were undoubtedly some people who, seeing those three crosses from a distance, thought that all three of the crucified men were robbers.

We have said that life in solidarity with the world provides the essential context for mission, that the opportunity for Christians to articulate the word of God's *shalom* comes not when we ask someone, "Are you saved?" but when someone asks us, "What are you getting out of this? What are you doing?" Solidarity with the world and participation in God's work in the world are prerequisite to verbal witness. This fact was demonstrated not only by my own experience in Berlin, but daily in East Germany when the Communists asked the young Christians, "Why haven't you died out yet?" Communist theory maintains that if Communism changes the face of society, and economic exploitation is abolished, the church will disappear. Communists believe the church is the guardian of the status quo. "We've done all this," say the Communists, "but you are still here. Why? Please explain to us why you haven't died out? What are you doing here?" This challenge provides the opportunity for a humble articulation of the only Word that we Christians have.

So far we have been considering illustrations of ministry or mission. It is now time for a more formal definition of ministry. It must be emphatically Christological.

Just as there is only *one* sacrament — not two or six or eighty-five — and that one is Jesus of Nazareth; and just as there is only *one* Word that God has and that one is the life of Jesus, to which we respond; so there is only *one* ministry, and that is the ministry of Jesus of Nazareth. We are given the privilege of taking part in this. We can be partners. We must therefore define what we mean by ministry, recalling what Jesus said about *his* ministry.

We find Jesus' definition of his ministry, and therefore of ours, in Luke 4, beginning with verse 16. Here Jesus, who has just reached adulthood, goes back to his home town and attends the synagogue.

> And he came to Nazareth, where he had been brought up; and he went to the synagogue, as his custom was, on the Sabbath day. And he stood up to read; and there was given to him the book of the prophet Isaiah. He opened the book and found the place where it was written, "The Spirit of the Lord is upon me, because he has anointed me [ordained me, selected me — and here is the ministry] to preach good news to the poor. He has sent me to proclaim release to the captives and recovering of sight to the blind, to set at liberty those who are oppressed, to proclaim the acceptable year of the Lord." And he closed the book, and gave it back to the attendant, and sat down; and the eyes of all in the synagogue were fixed on him. And he began to say to them, "Today this scripture has been fulfilled in your hearing."

All of the people spoke very well of him and said, "Isn't this Joseph's boy? Isn't it nice that one of our boys has made good and come back here?" They were all very well pleased, but only a few verses later something annoyed them so much that they chased Jesus out of town and were ready to pitch him off a cliff. Now, what did he say between this wonderful first impression and his narrow escape that annoyed people so?

Jesus said: "I tell you, there were many widows in Israel in the days of Elijah, when the heaven was shut up three years and six months, when there came a great famine over all the land; and Elijah was sent to none of them but only to Zarephath, in the land of Sidon, a woman who was a widow." God had worked through a nonbeliever, a non-Jew! *Very* annoying! "And there were many lepers in Israel in the time of the prophet Elisha; and none of them was cleansed, but only Naaman, the Syrian." God had showed his healing action to another nonbeliever. Can't we get *one* believer in the picture? No, that is the end of the sermon. "When they heard this, all in the synagogue were filled with wrath. And they rose up and put him out of the city, and led him to the brow of the hill on which their city was built, that they might throw him down headlong. But passing through the midst of them he went away."

The reason Jesus annoyed these people was that he insisted that God's ministry, the ministry in which he was participating, was *not* restricted to the believing community. It was effected through those who were despised, rejected, and outside; and this was too much even for those in his own home town to appreciate.

This is a sobering note on which to begin a formal definition of Christian ministry, but it is desperately essential today. Later on we shall discuss other images, in which God makes us his agents, servants, representatives, demonstrators, but we must begin by recognizing that he uses all sorts of people to do his work.

Another difficulty we face today is that one of the terms used most frequently for describing our ministry, "priesthood of all believers," is not adequate. We shall be suggesting some alternative images later. But, first of all, let us notice that the ministry of the church — that is, participation in the liberating, whole-making activity of Jesus of Nazareth as it continues into the present day — this ministry of the church is *not* something which belongs to one group within the church. It does not belong to those who have "Reverend" before their name, or who have been through some kind of ordination service complete with the laying on of hands. Such an idea would be pure clericalism. There is absolutely no evidence in the New Testament or anywhere else in the Bible that the ministry belongs to one group within the church, not even to so-called "full-time Christian workers." The ministry belongs to Jesus, and he allows all his people to share in it.

But let us return to the basic symbol. For us today, the most helpful image of the ministry is *not* the "priesthood of all believers." First of all, that term never appears in the New Testament; in fact Christians are referred to there as priests only two or three times. A far more frequent figure for describing the ministry of the church is that of the athlete, the soldier, the farmer, and even the servant. Here (2 Timothy 2:3-7) is a passage where these figures are all mixed together:

> Take your share of suffering as a good soldier of Christ Jesus. No soldier on service gets entangled in civilian pursuits, since his aim is to satisfy the one who enlisted him. An athlete is not crowned unless he competes according to

the rules. It is the hard-working farmer who ought to have the first share of the crops. Think over what I say, for the Lord will grant you understanding in everything.

As we read through the New Testament, we find that the figure of the soldier is used more frequently than any other to describe the life of the Christian in the world. He is a soldier when Paul says he should prepare himself with the full armor of God: the helmet of wholeness, with feet shod with the preparation of *shalom.* The very word "sacrament," which we have been discussing, was originally used to signify the oath which the Roman soldier took, the oath to obey his emperor, his commander-in-chief. Later the word "sacrament" was applied to baptism which was the pledge of the Christian soldier to serve *his* commander, Jesus. Still later it was applied to other things. It is interesting to note that the word "pagan" comes from the Latin word *paganus,* meaning one who was *not* in military service, a civilian. The soldiers of Jesus were distinguished from the *pagani,* from those who were engaged in civilian pursuits, and the title that the early church gave Jesus was thus that of a military commander-in-chief. He was the *kyrios,* the commander, the one who was responsible and who was to be obeyed in political and military decisions.

Because Jesus was their commander-in-chief, the Christians got into difficulty when they wouldn't put a pinch of incense on the altar of Caesar. Caesar also claimed to be the commander, the *kyrios.* The fact that Jesus and Caesar claimed the same title was politically dangerous. The person who acknowledged that the title belonged rightfully to Jesus immediately became a political insurrectionary. Not many of us have been arrested recently for refusing to put pinches of incense on anyone's altar, for this issue is dead; it no longer annoys the power structures. But how today can we make a confession which engages and challenges the political authority of our society as that one challenged the rulers of its own society?

"Jesus is the *kyrios*" — what does that statement mean today for the ministry? There was once a student who decided he would rewrite the whole New Testament using very modern language. Even *The New English Bible* sounded outmoded to him. He was especially concerned about the word "Lord." It is a feudal term, coming from a social order entirely different from ours, and there is no contemporary image back of it. "The house of the Lord" means nothing to us, but when this term was selected by the translators of the King James Version it had a real significance to people who knew what it meant in their daily lives to enter the house of the manorial lord. What word could this student find to describe Jesus, that would say the same thing to us today as the word "Lord" did to them? He tried various possibilities: Dean? That didn't seem right. Boss? That didn't quite click. Then he finally gave up; he couldn't find one.

What could we suggest? Perhaps the closest modern equivalent is the word "sovereign." The words "sovereign" and "sovereignty" are at least in the lexicon of modern political theory. "Sovereignty" signifies the authority to whom we owe highest allegiance, the authority who has the final say over us and over a particular place. The decision to say "Jesus Christ is *kyrios*," "Jesus is Lord," is really to say that he is the one to whom I owe my obedience — not the United States of America, not my personal whims, not my family, not my state, not my race; none of these things can claim my highest allegiance, for Jesus alone is my commander-in-chief.

We must concede immediately that there are some dangers in using this kind of military terminology. Some people have reasoned that if you have an army you must have not just privates and sergeants, but colonels and majors as well. So this imagery was taken over by the early church hierarchy and used to bolster its claims to tell the common Christians what to do. But this use of the figure was a misuse. The same image was misused by the Crusaders, who saw themselves as soldiers of Christ defeating the enemy with the sword. It was misused also during the Cromwell period, and it is still misused today. It need not be, however, for we can perceive the essential difference between the soldier of Christ and the soldier of Caesar as he appears in today's world. The soldier of Christ is the one who fights for *shalom*, who fights for peace. He is a commando of reconciliation. The difference between him and a soldier of Caesar is that, instead of shedding someone else's blood, he sheds his own. He pours himself out as a sacrifice. He dies in order to win. His victory is his defeat.

Now, let us move further into the figure of the army. Let us visualize the church — the people of God — as an army, one whose feet are shod with the preparation of the message of *shalom*, whose helmet is wholeness, and whose sword is truth. It is an army of those who are ready at any point to let themselves be poured out to participate in the reconciliation which is already being worked by Jesus. But what are the characteristics of such an army? These five elements may help describe it:

1. First of all, an army has to be *trained*. Student conferences and other church gatherings make sense only if they train soldiers to fight the battles they will find when they return to their various posts along the front. The reason why so many of our gatherings in the Christian church seem unnecessary and tedious today is that we are not engaged in the battle on the front. We do not see them as training.

A parachutist gets interested in training when he has to jump the next day. He'd better learn how the parachute operates if tomorrow he is going to bail out at 20,000 feet. For him the training session in which he learns the lay of the land where he is going to come down, how to move his body, and how to pull the cord — such a session is not boring at all. He has a certain existential interest in what is going on in such a training session. On the other hand, we are bored by *our* training sessions because we never jump. We don't jump into the place where we are needed for reconciliation, where we are needed to be poured out. Like the worst kind of soldiers, we hang around the barracks. There are many who think the finest service that a Christian student can render is to spend all the time he possibly can at the Baptist Student Center. If a soldier decided he would rather hang around the barracks than go out on the front and risk getting shot, however, he would not be commended. He would be court-martialed. We must discover some way at our denominational student centers to introduce a type of court-martial for those who spend too much time lounging around the barracks instead of getting out where the shooting is going on.

Can you imagine the commander-in-chief coming and asking us today, "How is the battle for *shalom* going on in the world?"

And someone would reply, "It is going on very well, General. Why, we just had 600 of the soldiers together. That is more than we have had together for a long time. The spirit was fine. The singing was marvelous."

He would say, "That's excellent, but what about the war? How is the war going on?"

"Well we just built three new, wonderful barracks on our campus, an excellent strategy consultation room, and a very fine weapon storage department."

You can imagine the general's reply. If we go on trying to convince ourselves that merely preparing and training and building the military facilities will be the way to get on with this war, we are defeating ourselves.

2. Second, the army of which we are a part must be flexible and mobile. It could be compared to *a guerilla army*, battling in small units of two and three persons here and there, sometimes as individuals fighting alone. We are not fighting against a world with which we are at enmity; rather, it is a world in which a victory has already been achieved. But there are still pockets of resistance where people don't know yet that the capital

has fallen. Because we are a guerilla army, we have to learn how to fight in small units and not always in a large platoon. We must sometimes meet clandestinely for our training.

3. Another thing that we could say about the army is that its soldiers, like those of any other army, must *learn to follow orders*. Now, in the Christian context, these are not the orders which are given by the clergy; they are the orders which arise from what Paul calls mutual submission. Here is where we see the absolute need in our church today to recover discipline, to find some way to make it costly for a person to enter the army of *shalom*. Once more my experience with East German Christians may illustrate what I mean. Here is a country in which it has become costly to be a Christian. Because of the fact that it is a Communist realm, having your name on a church roll no longer helps you in your advancement, nor gets you a promotion. In fact, the effect is just the opposite: If you are a Christian, you must be 20 to 25% better qualified than the next person, to get the same job. You take upon yourself a kind of permanent social disability.

Does this handicap mean that the intensity and depth of the Christian student community has been lessened? Quite the opposite! When I visited the University of Leipzig in February, 1963, I found four hundred students attending a Bible study session on one evening. The East German students are not interested in hayrides or doggy roasts. They are interested in training sessions which prepare them to fight a tough battle. They study the Bible and they study Karl Marx, because they want to know both about the faith they confess and about the world in which they confess it.

4. Fourth, an army has to be *supplied and fed.* Here we come to the function of a group which never really gets to the front line but makes it possible for the fighting force to do its job. Call this group the clergy, if you will, though "clergy" is a wretched term. There are better ones, such as "the servants of the servants of God" or "the kitchen troops of the army of the Lord." Those whom we call clergy give no orders; they supply the food and weapons that are needed. They may have something to do with the training and strategy sessions, but the real fighting is done by those who go out from the base to the front line. An army does have to be supplied, and we do need the people who are engaged in the training and supplying and preparation of the army of the Lord. Anyone thinking of this work as a career, as one type of service in the army, shouldn't be deterred by the fact that everybody is a minister in today's concept of ministry. One who has been to a theological seminary or been ordained can't claim to be the only minister. All any of us can say is that we have rediscovered the principles of mutual submission in the army. You have your job; someone else has his; I have mine. "There are varieties of gifts, but the same Spirit" (1 Corinthians 12:3).

There is no place for a priestly hierarchy in the church. There is no evidence in the New Testament for a priesthood; in fact, Jesus himself steadfastly refused to be called "priest." Even if we call men pastors or reverends or something else, there is no place for a permanent, established clerical class or for an elite of religious specialists. In view of all this, how do we explain the fact that we have become a clericalized church despite the heritage of our fathers and the evidence of the New Testament? How do we explain the fact that we do have a permanent clergy who in some sense feel themselves superior to, or at least in a status higher than, the laity? How can we learn to stop using that terrible phrase, "I am only a layman"?

These are tough questions. We have to do something rather desperate in the form of deep surgery. Perhaps what we need is an inflation of ordination. Should we ordain everyone who intends that his life shall be lived as a servant of Jesus Christ? Should we stop limiting ordination to people who are going to be paid by the church, or people who have been to a theological seminary? Should we ordain all those who see their whole life as participation in the army of *shalom,* whether as a nurse or a teacher or a diplomat or a lawyer? Perhaps we should ordain them, but on the other hand we must remember that baptism is already an ordination.

Baptism is already a "sacrament," an oath, a way by which we are brought into the army of *shalom.* So it might make even more sense to ordain no one. Many New Testament scholars believe there was no group in the New Testament church which was specially "ordained" in our sense of the word. We must question whether we are right in ordaining people to a special group. We must ask whether the Protestant rite of ordination, which is becoming more and more like the ordination of a priest, does not symbolize a whole different theology of the church from that of the New Testament. Perhaps we ought to do away with it for a while and go back to being a church of the laity *in toto.*

We need radical measures. Some people have asked me why I always cross out the word "Reverend" on my badge at conferences. I cross it out because I am fighting, along with a few other hardy souls, a battle against this terrible title, and I invite all who at one time have had hands laid upon their heads in a cultic rite of ordination to join me. Let us have done with this title, "Reverend," which (besides being nonbiblical) claims a distinction to which we have no right. Who would really claim that we are more to be "revered" than the kids we've heard about who have risked their lives for their beliefs in Selma or Birmingham? Radical steps are needed to create a *total* ministry and not simply a ministerial elite.

5. One more thing to be said about an army is that its soldiers are *sent to where the fight is going on.* The battle is fought along different lines in different ages — now here, next year there, and in the future somewhere else. The soldiers are sent precisely where the brokenness of their fellowmen precipitates the battle for reconciliation at the particular time. For this reason we need not apologize today for an emphasis on racial reconciliation in the United States of America. This happens to be where the battle is going on today. To complain that there has been overemphasis on this particular front would be like calling up General Eisenhower from Dover Beach or from the Normandy beachhead on D-Day and saying, "Aren't you throwing a few too many

troops in here, General? Why don't you send a few down to southern France or Spain, or maybe over to Ireland?"

The fact was that the shooting happened to be going on at Normandy beachhead, and this is where the troops were sent. We make no apologies for the fact that at different points in history we are called and sent to different locations on the front, and that as Christians consulting together we can pick out where this front is and then send ourselves in.

This is not to say that the only front on which Christians are sent to be agents of reconciliation, soldiers of *shalom* today, is the front of racial integration. It is the most important one, but there are others. There is the struggle of the cold war, where we have to consider how we can be agents of reconciliation between two gigantic power blocs armed for mutual annihilation. How can we begin to pour ourselves out in trying to effect reconciliation here? On another front, we have to think of the schism in our nation and in our world between the rich and the poor. How can we begin to bridge this gap? We have to think of the tragic and embarrassing barrier between the sexes which we encounter every day. How can we be human across this wall? How can we be an agent of reconciliation to our girlfriend or boyfriend? How can we be a messenger of *shalom* whose activity and attitude affirm the humanity of the other person rather than use him or her for our own ends? What about the tragic breach between the generations — the one that students feel every time they go home for a Christmas or an Easter holiday?

How can we be agents of reconciliation across the barrier? All these are important fronts.

This means that Christians will be sent to the very places where it is dangerous to be today, where a reconciliatory role may bring unpopularity, ridicule, and derogation. If you are not getting shot at, you can be pretty sure that you are not on the firing line where the new ministry is going on.

We find ourselves as soldiers of *shalom* in what might be compared to a revolutionary crisis. In every successful revolution there comes a point at which the new revolutionary regime has taken power, but the old regime has not surrendered, and therefore there is an overlap of claims to ultimate sovereignty and authority. It is at this point of overlap that we find ourselves. The early Christians saw Jesus of Nazareth as the one who is already in command, who has been given ultimate sovereignty to the world: "God has made him both Lord and Christ, this Jesus whom you crucified" (Acts 2:36). But there are many other groups claiming our sovereignty, claiming our obedience. This is the interim situation in which we find ourselves. Here is the way Paul puts it in 2 Corinthians 5: "And he died for all, that those who live might live no longer for themselves but for him. . . ." With us, therefore, worldly standards have ceased to count in our estimate of any man; that is, the standards, the rules, the laws of the regime which are now being replaced have ceased to count. Even if once they counted in our understanding of Christ, they do so no longer. When anyone is in Christ, there is a new regime, a new world, a new order. The old order has gone and the new has already begun. Christ has reconciled us to himself and has enlisted us in this service of reconciliation.

Once in the state of Georgia there were two governors, each claiming to be sovereign authority in this very sovereign state. One of them had a desk in the governor's office and the other set himself up in the hall. Each of them gave orders to the state police. This disputed claim to the authority placed a decision on every citizen of Georgia and more especially on every state policeman. Each had to make up his mind whether to obey Governor Talmadge or Governor Arnall. This dilemma provides a parallel to our situation as Christians today. We already live in the new order, which has begun to file claims on our obedience. But we are confronted daily by the old authorities even though they have been defeated by the revolutionary regime. We are not building the kingdom of God. It has already been established, the victory has been won, and we are simply privileged to participate in the fruits of the new regime. But because the old regime still makes claims, our participation in the fruits of the new may get us into trouble.

This is about as far as one can go in applying military terminology to the new ministry. There is only one ministry — the ministry of Jesus, a revolutionary ministry — and it is into this ministry that we are called to participate. It all goes back to the point made in the first chapter about loving the world in which we have been placed, loving it enough to sacrifice for it, taking it with life-and-death seriousness, sticking with it even when the going is rough. Our commitment to the renewal of the world means we are willing to stand with the world in which God has placed us — loving it when it despises us, serving it when it doesn't appreciate us, being available to it when it turns its back on us. At a conference in a very beautiful setting just outside Berlin, a group of students from various East German universities had gathered. They were in a happy holiday mood because they had just finished their semester's work. It was also a sad time because I was leaving these good friends to go back to the United States, and in a world like ours no one could know whether we would ever see each other again. We began talking about an incident which had aroused the entire population, concerning a Communist-sponsored peace rally in Helsinki. A delegation of sixty-two young East Germans had been very carefully selected from the most dependable Communist youth to attend this rally. They were area and district leaders of the Communist youth organization, people whose fervor and dedication had been proved by their having achieved high office in this organization. Yet thirty-six of the sixty-two did not return, but left and went to West Germany. This defection created an enormous scandal in East Germany. The heads of the regime demanded the resignation (though not the arrest) of the secretary of the youth organization. Decrying the lack of patriotism, and dedication of these opportunists, they asked that the whole place be housecleaned.

When I discussed this event with this group of young Christians, one of them said something which at first came as a shock. But the more I have thought about it the more I understand it. It may help us to understand our responsibility and our relationship to our campuses and our society. This East German Christian said: "Yes, that was really very shocking about those Communists, that over half of them didn't come back. If that had been sixty-two of us Christians who had been sent up to Helsinki, we would *all* have come back. That is the difference between us and them. We love this country. We're here to serve it and to love it, but they're here to get out of it what they can. We have to love this country because nobody else does. That's our *job* as Christians here in East Germany."

Their job as Christians in East Germany is also our job as Christians in our own country. Wherever we are, it is our job to love the world that God loves, to serve it when it despises us, to come back to it and to be with it, to be there as representatives of the *shalom* which God is making possible for all his people.